Folding
PAPER
AIRPLANES
with STEM

For Beginners to Experts

by Marie Buckingham

CAPSTONE PRESS
a capstone imprint

TABLE OF
CONTENTS

Advanced-Level Projects...........58

Expert-Level Projects **82**

Get ready to leave the ground behind . . .

It's time to fold and fly!

Packed with more than 30 projects, *Folding Paper Airplanes with STEM* has models for everyone. Know the basics but want to challenge yourself? Got it. Been folding for a while and want to try something fresh? Got that too. And if you've never folded a paper airplane before? Follow the book from start to finish to make the journey from your first day of flight school to your first solo flight.

A few things to note before diving in:

- Check the lightbulb boxes tucked alongside the project instructions for bite-sized explanations of flight-science concepts related to your models.

- Check the photo boxes for tips on how to best launch your finished planes.

- Remember, there are four main forces that airplanes need to fly successfully: lift, weight, thrust, and drag. But the paper airplanes in this book need one more thing: YOU!

MATERIALS

Every paper airplane builder needs a well-stocked toolbox. The models in this book use the materials listed below. Take a minute before you begin folding to gather what you need:

Paper

Any paper you can fold will work. Notebook paper is always popular, but paper with cool colors and designs gives your planes style.

Scissors

Keep a pair of scissors handy. Some models need a snip here or there to fly well.

Paper Clips

Paper clips are perfect for adding weight to a plane's nose. Keep a supply of small and large paper clips on hand.

Clear Tape

Most paper airplanes don't need tape, but when they do, you'll be glad you have it ready to go.

Rubber Bands

Rubber bands can send some airplane models sailing. Long, thin rubber bands work well.

Small Binder Clips

Like paper clips, small binder clips can add weight to a plane's nose.

TECHNIQUES AND TERMS

Folding paper airplanes isn't difficult when you understand common folding techniques and terms. Review this list before folding the models in this book. Remember to refer back to this list if you get stuck on a tricky step.

Valley Folds

Valley folds are represented by a dashed line. The paper is creased along the line. The top surface of the paper is folded against itself like a book.

Mountain Folds

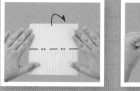

Mountain folds are represented by a pink or white dashed and dotted line. The paper is creased along the line and folded behind.

Reverse Folds

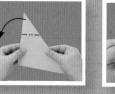

Reverse folds are made by opening a pocket slightly and folding the model inside itself along existing creases.

Mark Folds

Mark folds are light folds used to make reference creases for a later step. Ideally, a mark fold will not be seen in the finished model.

Rabbit Ear Folds

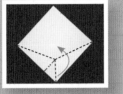  

Rabbit ear folds are formed by bringing two edges of a point together using existing creases. The new point is folded to one side.

Squash Folds

Squash folds are formed by lifting one edge of a pocket and reforming it so the spine gets flattened. The existing creases become new edges.

FOLDING SYMBOLS

Fold the paper in the direction of the arrow.

Fold the paper behind.

Fold the paper and then unfold it.

Turn the paper over or rotate it to a new position.

A fold or edge hidden under another layer of paper; also used to mark where to cut with a scissors

BEGINNING-LEVEL PROJECTS

Welcome to flight school! Almost every paper airplane starts with a fold. (The second project in this section, the Spinning Blimp, is one of the few that doesn't.)

The following nine projects are designed to introduce you to the most basic paper airplane folds. Take your time, keep your creases sharp, and practice, practice, practice. The skills you learn here will be key to helping you fly the most amazing planes in the sky!

DYNAMIC DART

Traditional Model

The Dynamic Dart is one of the most popular paper planes on the planet. It's the type of model that never lets you down. Best of all, its steps are super simple. You'll be folding it from memory in no time at all.

Materials

* 8.5- by 11-inch (22- by 28-centimeter) paper

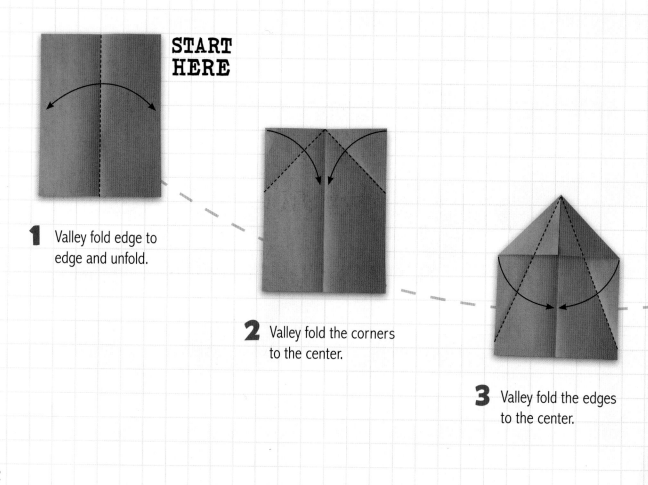

START HERE

1 Valley fold edge to edge and unfold.

2 Valley fold the corners to the center.

3 Valley fold the edges to the center.

END HERE

7 Finished Dynamic Dart

Airplanes move forward in flight because of a force called thrust. The push of a hand provides the thrust needed for most paper airplanes to fly. Some models use a launcher with a large rubber band that is pulled back and snapped to provide a quick burst of thrust. Real airplanes get their thrust from gas- or electric-powered engines.

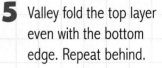

6 Lift the wings.

5 Valley fold the top layer even with the bottom edge. Repeat behind.

4 Mountain fold the model in half and rotate.

FLYING TIP

Use a medium throw with a slight upward angle.

SPINNING BLIMP

Traditional Model

The Spinning Blimp is a clever paper toy. In your hand, it looks like a ribbon. But in the air, it spins so fast that it looks like a tiny blimp. Release it as high as you can and watch it twirl.

Materials

* 8.5- by 11-inch (22- by 28-cm) paper
* scissors

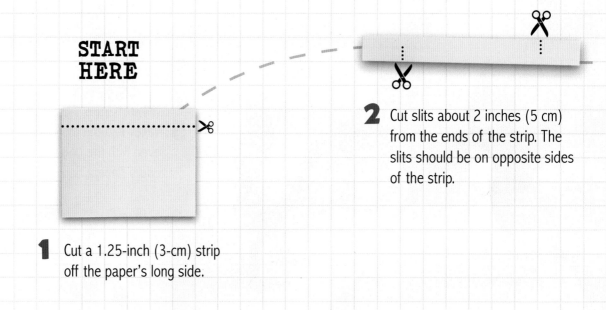

START HERE

1 Cut a 1.25-inch (3-cm) strip off the paper's long side.

2 Cut slits about 2 inches (5 cm) from the ends of the strip. The slits should be on opposite sides of the strip.

FLYING TIP

Pinch one side of the model's loop with your index finger and thumb. Release with a gentle forward push.

4 Slide the slits together to form a loop.

3 Bend the strip to bring the two slits together.

5 Finished Spinning Blimp

END HERE

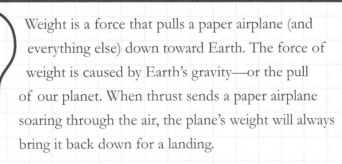

Weight is a force that pulls a paper airplane (and everything else) down toward Earth. The force of weight is caused by Earth's gravity—or the pull of our planet. When thrust sends a paper airplane soaring through the air, the plane's weight will always bring it back down for a landing.

WHIRLY

Traditional Model

How can a simple paper strip be so much fun? With two small folds, the Whirly looks like a useless scrap of paper. But launch it once and you'll want to watch it flutter to the floor over and over again.

Materials

* 8.5- by 11-inch (22- by 28-cm) paper
* scissors

START HERE

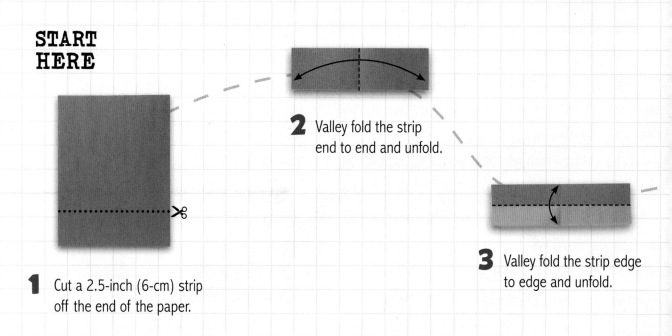

1 Cut a 2.5-inch (6-cm) strip off the end of the paper.

2 Valley fold the strip end to end and unfold.

3 Valley fold the strip edge to edge and unfold.

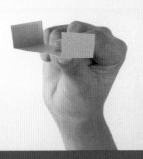

Pinch the middle of the model with your index finger and thumb. Release with a gentle forward push. The higher you hold it, the longer it will flutter.

6 Finished Whirly

END HERE

5 Valley fold the ends of one small rectangle. Allow these flaps to stand up at 90-degree angles.

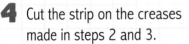

4 Cut the strip on the creases made in steps 2 and 3.

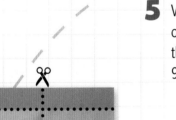

As an airplane moves forward through the sky, a force called drag pushes against it. Tiny air molecules rub against the plane and cause drag. Drag always works in the opposite direction of a moving object.

RING WING

Traditional Model

The Ring Wing looks more like a napkin ring than a paper airplane. But this circular glider really sails.

Materials

* 6-inch (15-cm) square of paper

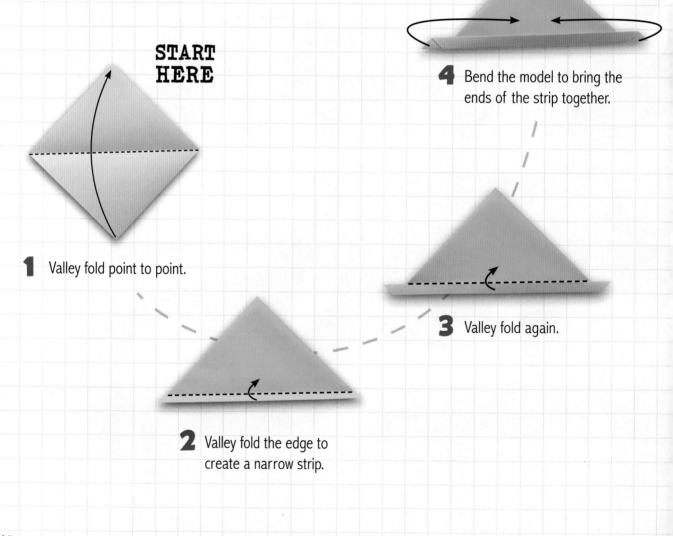

START HERE

1 Valley fold point to point.

2 Valley fold the edge to create a narrow strip.

3 Valley fold again.

4 Bend the model to bring the ends of the strip together.

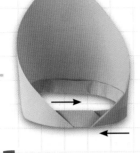

5 Tuck one end of the strip inside the other as far as it will go.

Hold the pointed end of the wing with your index finger and thumb. Release the Ring Wing with a gentle, forward push. Hold it high when you launch it to make it glide farther.

If something is streamlined, it has smooth edges, with few parts sticking out. Airplanes are streamlined. They have round, smooth noses and wheels that tuck inside the plane when in flight to reduce the amount of drag.

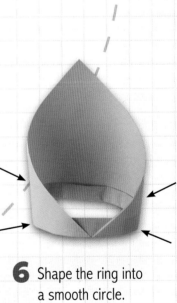

6 Shape the ring into a smooth circle.

7 Finished Ring Wing

END HERE

FLYING SQUIRREL

Traditional Model

This glider is nothing more than a single wing. But gravity and air currents give it amazing flights. With the right push, the model will glide like a graceful flying squirrel.

Materials

* 6-inch (15-cm) square of paper

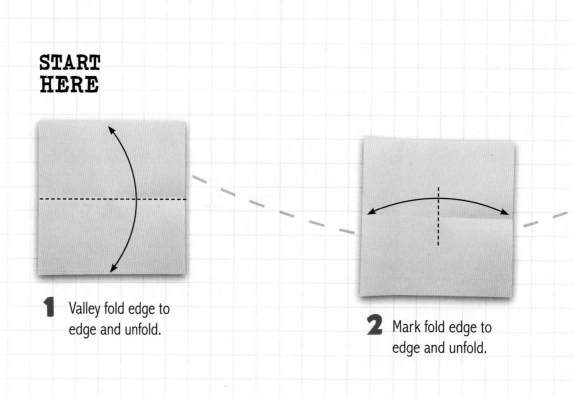

START HERE

1 Valley fold edge to edge and unfold.

2 Mark fold edge to edge and unfold.

4 Valley fold the corners to the center and unfold.

5 Reverse fold on the crease formed in step 4.

3 Valley fold the edge to the mark fold made in step 2.

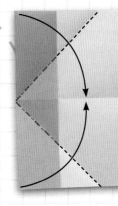

6 Valley fold the point.

Airplanes need lift to fly. As a plane soars into the air, its wings are angled slightly up. Air flowing underneath the bottom of the wing creates pressure. Air moving over the top of the wing speeds up and causes pressure to decrease. Since the pressure below the wing is greater than the pressure above, the pressure difference pushes up against the wings and creates lift.

Continue ▶

8 Mountain fold the model in half and unfold.

9 Finished Flying Squirrel

END
HERE

7 Valley fold the flaps and tuck them into the pockets of the point.

FLYING TIP

Pinch the back end of the wing with your index finger and thumb. Release with a gentle, forward push. The higher you hold it at launch, the farther it will glide.

H LICOPT R

Traditional Model

With a snip here and a fold there, you'll make the paper Helicopter in less than three minutes. This classic toy never ceases to amaze. Go ahead, give it a whirl!

Materials

* 8.5- by 11-inch (22- by 28-cm) paper
* scissors
* large paper clip

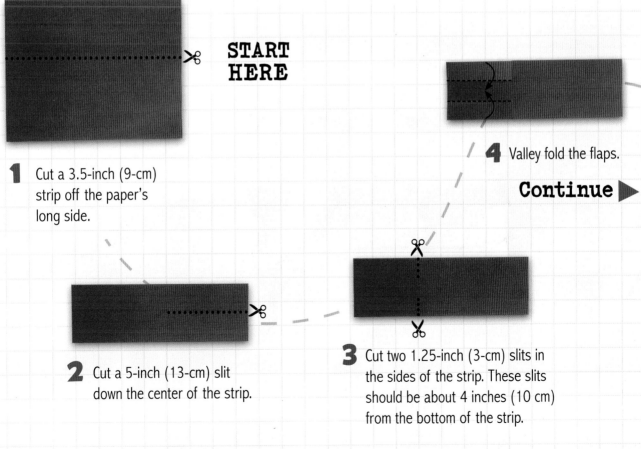

START HERE

1 Cut a 3.5-inch (9-cm) strip off the paper's long side.

2 Cut a 5-inch (13-cm) slit down the center of the strip.

3 Cut two 1.25-inch (3-cm) slits in the sides of the strip. These slits should be about 4 inches (10 cm) from the bottom of the strip.

4 Valley fold the flaps.

Continue ▶

6 Add a paper clip to the folded edge.

5 Valley fold the bottom edge.

7 Valley fold one propeller. Mountain fold the other propeller.

The main rotor on top of a helicopter works like a wing of an airplane. The difference is that the main rotor turns to create airflow, whereas airplane wings rely on the entire plane to move through the air. As air flows over and under the rotor, the pressure created on the bottom of the rotor is higher than the pressure on top. The higher pressure under the rotor pushes up and creates lift.

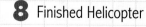

END HERE

8 Finished Helicopter

TAILSPIN

Traditional Model

Some paper airplanes land smoothly. But the Tailspin prefers crash landings. With a hard throw, this model spins wildly through the air and crashes in a blaze of glory.

Materials

* 8.5- by 11-inch (22- by 28-cm) paper

Continue ▶

START HERE

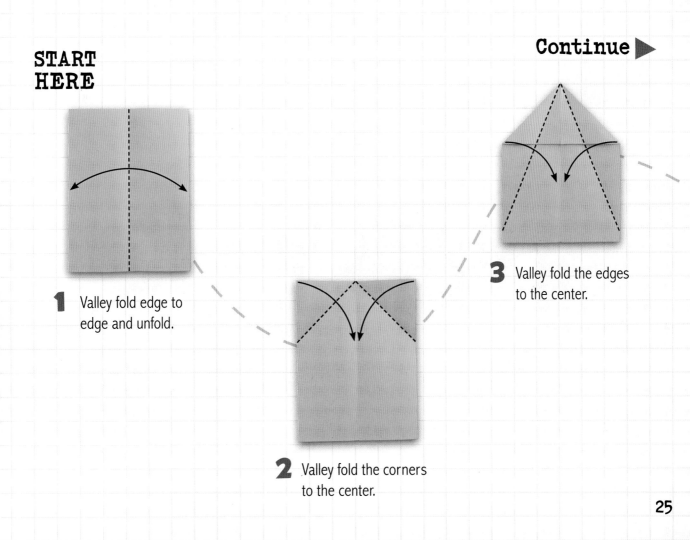

1 Valley fold edge to edge and unfold.

2 Valley fold the corners to the center.

3 Valley fold the edges to the center.

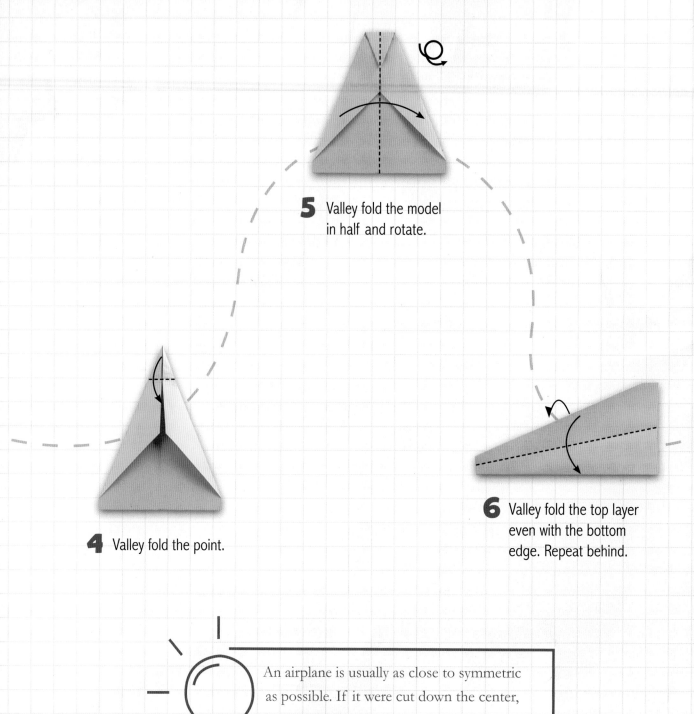

5 Valley fold the model in half and rotate.

4 Valley fold the point.

6 Valley fold the top layer even with the bottom edge. Repeat behind.

An airplane is usually as close to symmetric as possible. If it were cut down the center, length-wise, both sides would be almost exactly the same. Being symmetric helps to create a smooth, straight flight. The Tailspin model has one flap folded up and the other folded down. This asymmetric design sends the plane into a spin.

Use a strong throw with a slight upward angle.

7 Lift the wings.

8 Valley fold one corner up slightly. Mountain fold the other corner down slightly.

9 Finished Tailspin

END
HERE

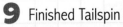

LONG RANGER

Traditional Model

The Long Ranger has no equal. It flies farther and straighter than any other model in this book. With the right throw, it can cover distances of 45 feet (14 meters). That's something to remember when your school has a paper airplane contest!

Materials

* 8.5- by 11-inch (22- by 28-cm) paper

START HERE

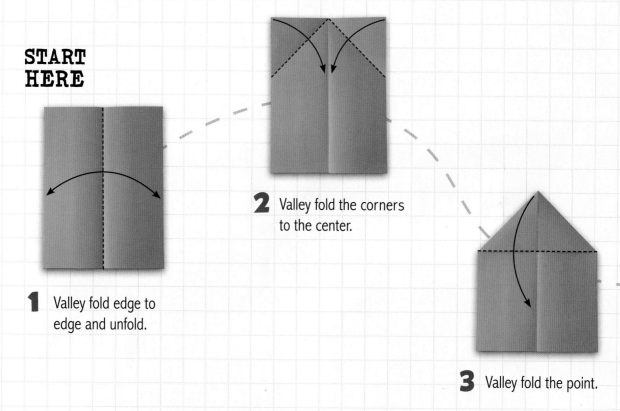

1 Valley fold edge to edge and unfold.

2 Valley fold the corners to the center.

3 Valley fold the point.

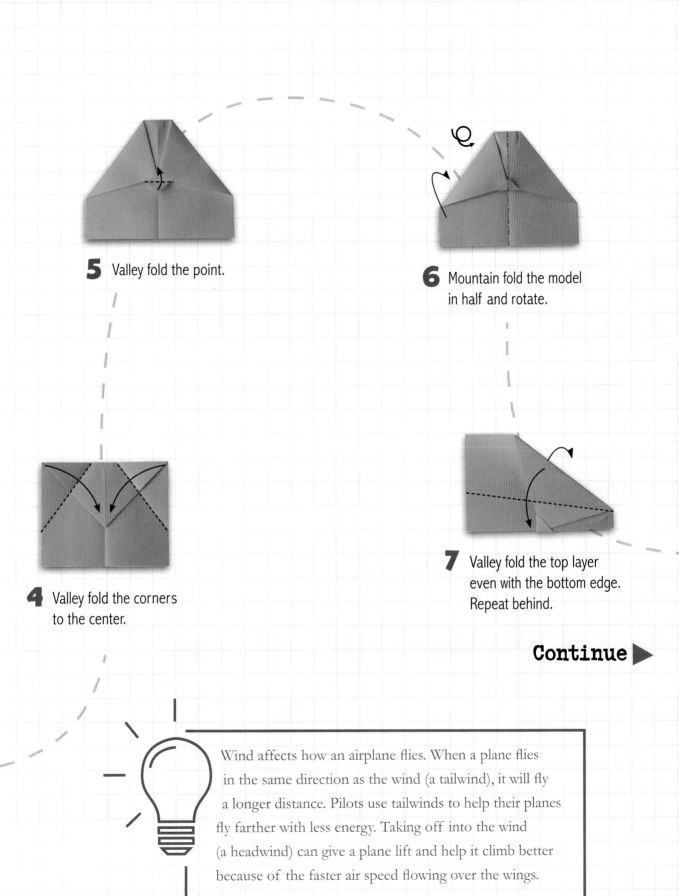

5 Valley fold the point.

6 Mountain fold the model in half and rotate.

4 Valley fold the corners to the center.

7 Valley fold the top layer even with the bottom edge. Repeat behind.

Continue ▶

Wind affects how an airplane flies. When a plane flies in the same direction as the wind (a tailwind), it will fly a longer distance. Pilots use tailwinds to help their planes fly farther with less energy. Taking off into the wind (a headwind) can give a plane lift and help it climb better because of the faster air speed flowing over the wings.

END HERE

9 Finished Long Ranger

8 Lift the wings.

FLYING TIP

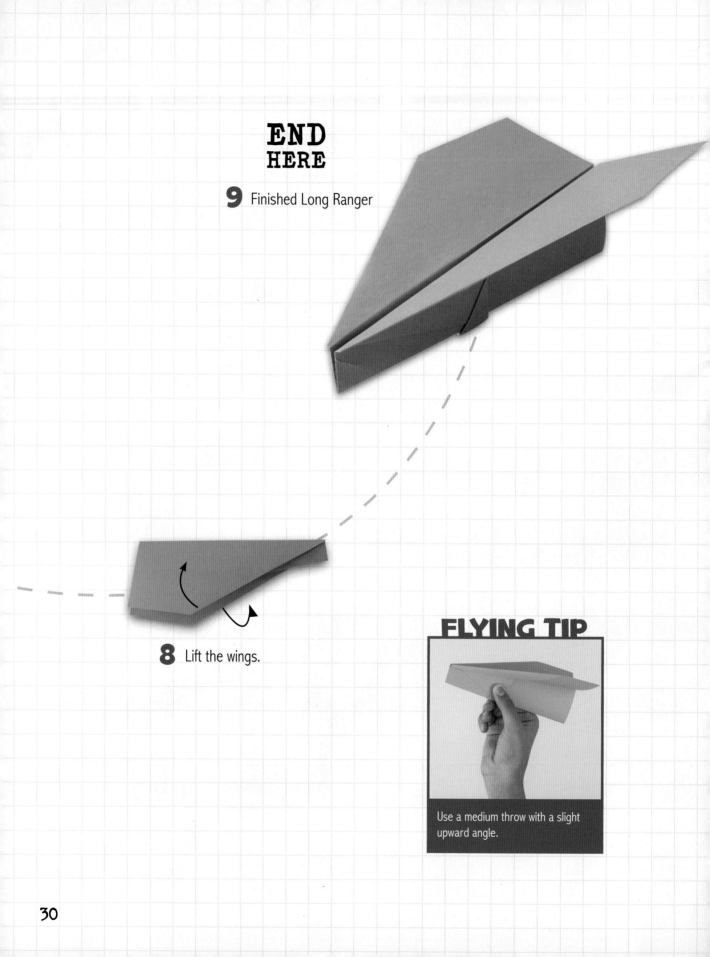

Use a medium throw with a slight upward angle.

ELEVATOR GLIDER

Traditional Model

If you like to tinker with flight patterns, the Elevator Glider is just for you. Adjust the angles of the flaps to find the flight that you like.

Materials

* 8.5- by 11-inch (22- by 28-cm) paper
* scissors

START HERE

1 Valley fold edge to edge and unfold.

2 Valley fold the corners to the center. Note how the creases end at the bottom corners of the paper.

Continue ▶

3 Valley fold in half and unfold.

31

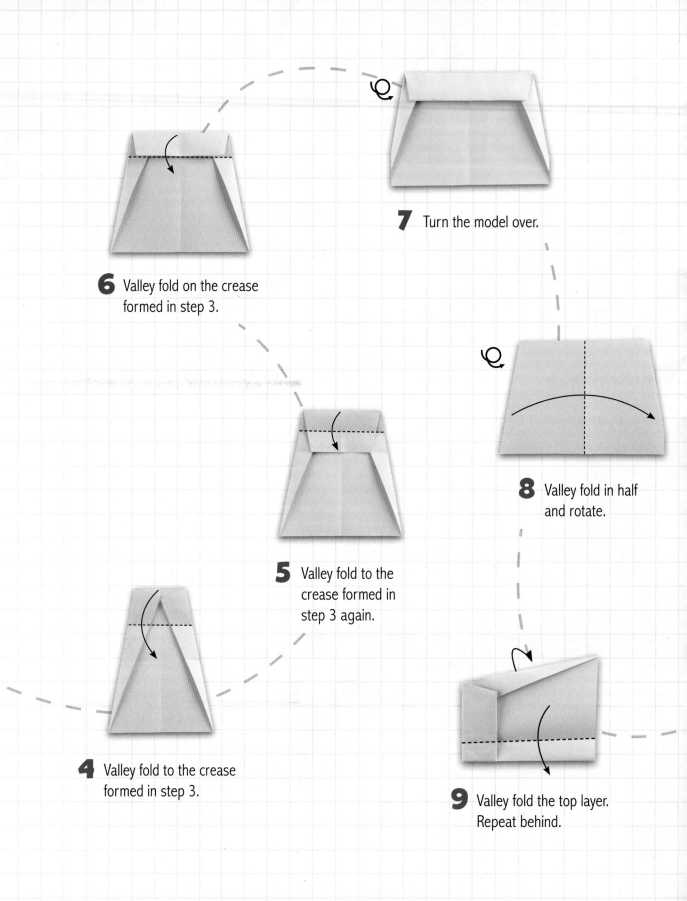

6 Valley fold on the crease formed in step 3.

7 Turn the model over.

8 Valley fold in half and rotate.

5 Valley fold to the crease formed in step 3 again.

4 Valley fold to the crease formed in step 3.

9 Valley fold the top layer. Repeat behind.

Flaps change the flow of air around an airplane and the direction of air forces pushing on it. A plane with flaps folded up on the back creates a force pushing down on the tail, which lifts the front. That's why the movable surface on the tail is called an elevator—it can cause up or down movement, just like an elevator!

10 Lift the wings.

11 Cut a flap in the back of each wing. Angle the flaps upward slightly.

12 Finished Elevator Glider

END HERE

NOVICE-LEVEL PROJECTS

Welcome to the cockpit! You've passed flight school and earned your seat next to the pilot. Now it's time to get a feel for those flight controls. The eight paper airplane projects in this section build on basic skills and challenge you to push your folds a bit further.

You'll have the chance to play with wing flaps and see what effect they have on a plane's flight. You'll even fold a swooping monoplane called the Vampire Bat!

AIR SHARK

Traditional Model

Prowl the skies with your very own Air Shark.
This sturdy plane has a smooth, steady glide.
It's a paper predator that's always ready to hunt.

Materials

* 8.5- by 11-inch (22- by 28-cm) paper

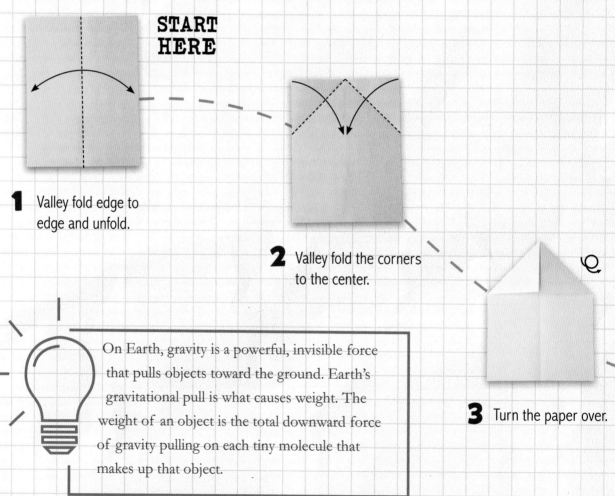

START HERE

1 Valley fold edge to edge and unfold.

2 Valley fold the corners to the center.

3 Turn the paper over.

On Earth, gravity is a powerful, invisible force that pulls objects toward the ground. Earth's gravitational pull is what causes weight. The weight of an object is the total downward force of gravity pulling on each tiny molecule that makes up that object.

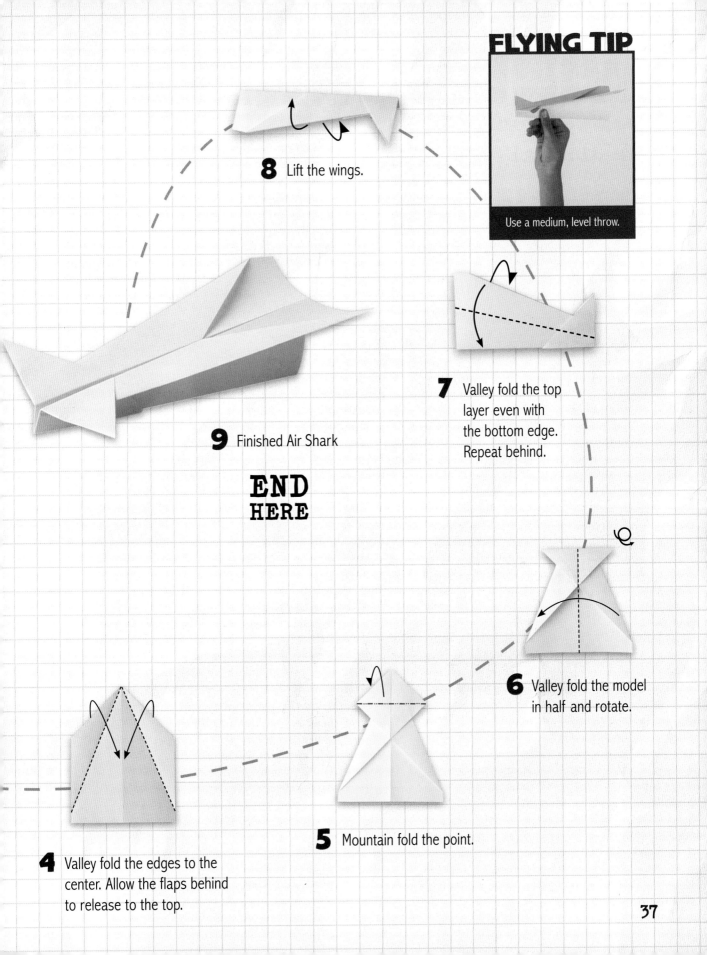

Use a medium, level throw.

8 Lift the wings.

9 Finished Air Shark

END HERE

7 Valley fold the top layer even with the bottom edge. Repeat behind.

6 Valley fold the model in half and rotate.

5 Mountain fold the point.

4 Valley fold the edges to the center. Allow the flaps behind to release to the top.

WIND TUNNEL

Traditional Model

The Wind Tunnel takes paper airplanes in a very
different direction. This circular wing is thrown like
a football. Get your arm warmed up. You'll be amazed
by how far this tube will glide through the air.

Materials

* 8.5- by 11-inch (22- by 28-cm) paper
* scissors
* tape

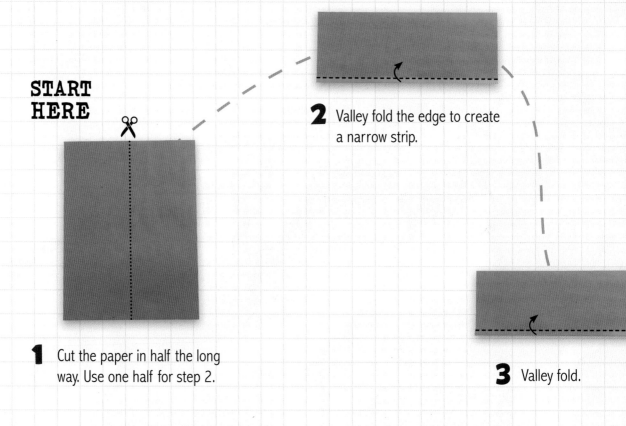

START HERE

1 Cut the paper in half the long way. Use one half for step 2.

2 Valley fold the edge to create a narrow strip.

3 Valley fold.

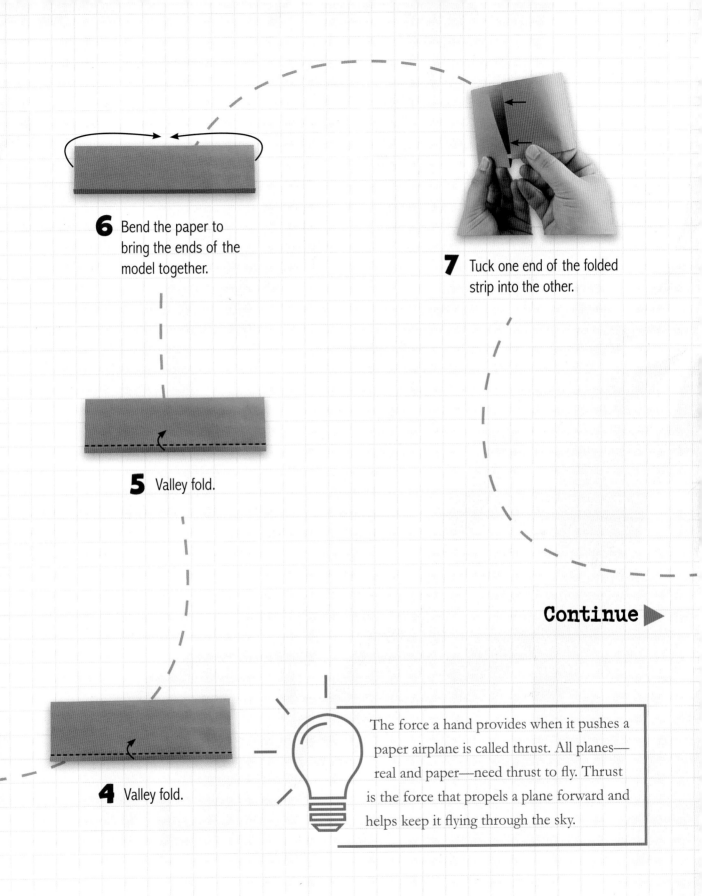

6 Bend the paper to bring the ends of the model together.

7 Tuck one end of the folded strip into the other.

5 Valley fold.

Continue ▶

4 Valley fold.

The force a hand provides when it pushes a paper airplane is called thrust. All planes—real and paper—need thrust to fly. Thrust is the force that propels a plane forward and helps keep it flying through the sky.

9 Shape the tube into a smooth circle.

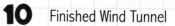

10 Finished Wind Tunnel

END HERE

8 Tape the seam to hold the model together.

FLYING TIP

Cup the model in your hand with the folded strip facing forward. Use a hard spiral throw as if you were throwing a football.

STREAKING EAGLE

Traditional Model

The Streaking Eagle combines style and mechanics. Sleek wing flaps help the plane fly straight. Elevators let you control how the plane rises or dives.

Materials

* 8.5- by 11-inch (22- by 28-cm) paper
* scissors

Continue ▶

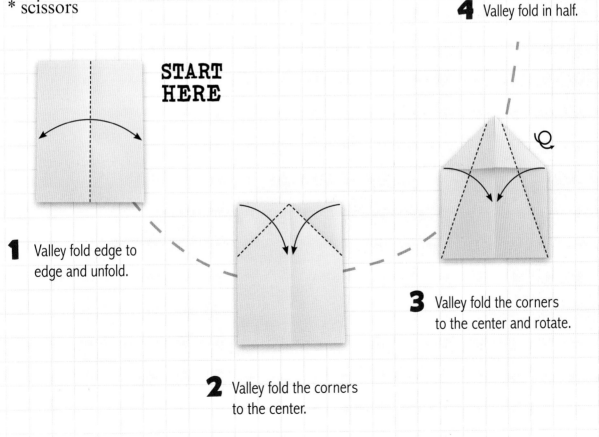

4 Valley fold in half.

1 Valley fold edge to edge and unfold.

START HERE

2 Valley fold the corners to the center.

3 Valley fold the corners to the center and rotate.

During flight, a pilot controls the movable surface on an airplane's tail called an elevator. The elevator moves an airplane's nose up or down. When the elevator is pushed down, the airplane's nose will move down. When the elevator is pulled up, the aircraft's nose will move up.

5 Valley fold the top layer. Repeat behind.

6 Valley fold the edge of the wing. Repeat behind.

7 Lift the wings.

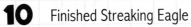

10 Finished Streaking Eagle

END HERE

9 Cut a flap in the back of each wing. Angle the flaps (elevators) upward slightly.

8 Lift the wing flaps so they stand up at 90-degree angles.

FLYING TIP

Use a medium, level throw. Adjust the flaps to control the flight path.

WHISPER DART

Designed by Christopher L. Harbo

The Whisper Dart looks like a simple paper airplane. But extra folds give it added weight in the nose. Got your eye on a target across the room? This design will deliver!

Materials

* 8.5- by 11-inch (22- by 28-cm) paper

START HERE

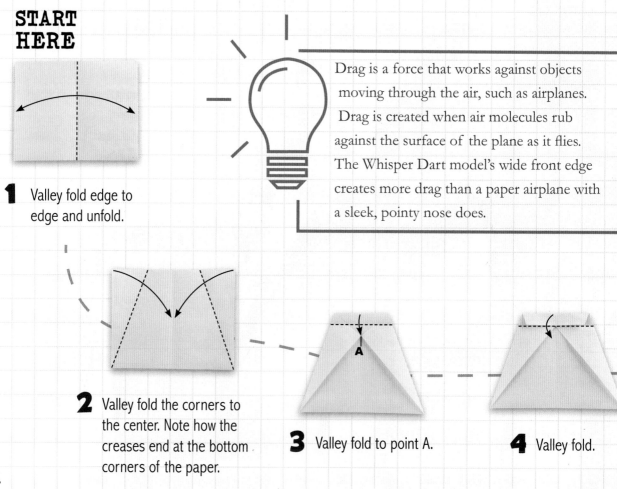

Drag is a force that works against objects moving through the air, such as airplanes. Drag is created when air molecules rub against the surface of the plane as it flies. The Whisper Dart model's wide front edge creates more drag than a paper airplane with a sleek, pointy nose does.

1 Valley fold edge to edge and unfold.

2 Valley fold the corners to the center. Note how the creases end at the bottom corners of the paper.

3 Valley fold to point A.

4 Valley fold.

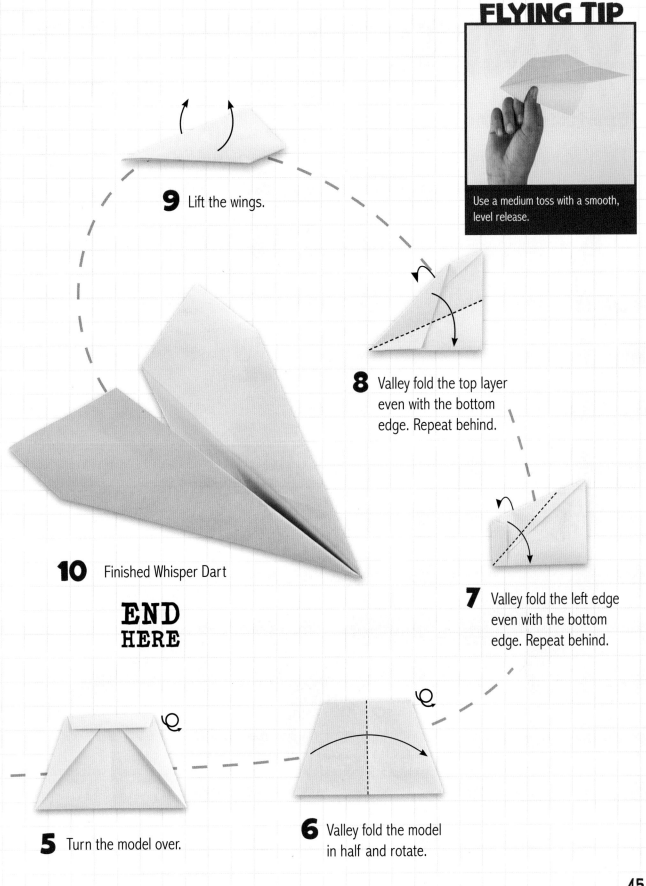

Use a medium toss with a smooth, level release.

9 Lift the wings.

8 Valley fold the top layer even with the bottom edge. Repeat behind.

7 Valley fold the left edge even with the bottom edge. Repeat behind.

10 Finished Whisper Dart

END HERE

5 Turn the model over.

6 Valley fold the model in half and rotate.

45

VAMPIRE BAT

Traditional Model

The Vampire Bat's flight path is a jaw-dropper. This amazing wing soars and swoops when thrown correctly. Folding it is easy. Finding a room large enough to fly it in may be a challenge.

Materials

* 8.5- by 11-inch (22- by 28-cm) paper

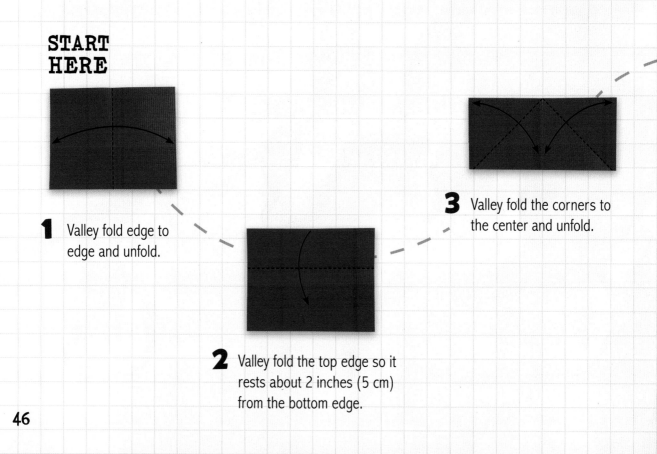

START HERE

1 Valley fold edge to edge and unfold.

2 Valley fold the top edge so it rests about 2 inches (5 cm) from the bottom edge.

3 Valley fold the corners to the center and unfold.

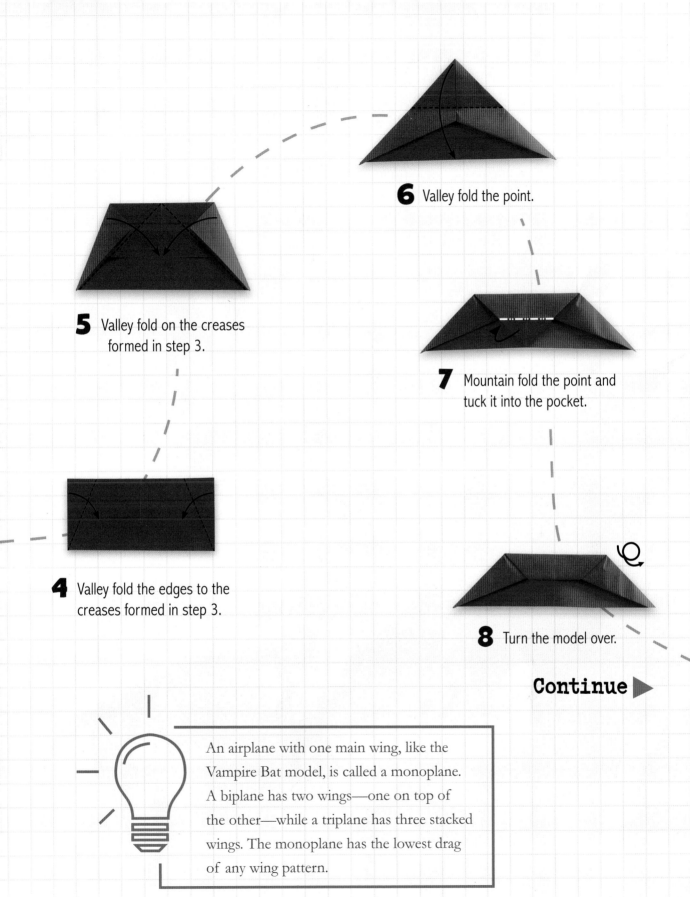

6 Valley fold the point.

5 Valley fold on the creases
formed in step 3.

7 Mountain fold the point and
tuck it into the pocket.

4 Valley fold the edges to the
creases formed in step 3.

8 Turn the model over.

Continue ▶

An airplane with one main wing, like the
Vampire Bat model, is called a monoplane.
A biplane has two wings—one on top of
the other—while a triplane has three stacked
wings. The monoplane has the lowest drag
of any wing pattern.

Pinch the back of the wing with two fingers and your thumb so the model forms a "V." Raise the model above your head and release with a strong forward flick of the wrist.

END HERE

11 Finished Vampire Bat

9 Mountain fold the wings and unfold slightly.

10 Valley fold the wing tips and unfold slightly.

ARROWHEAD

Traditional Model

Get ready to soar! The Arrowhead is a flying champion. This plane can cover amazing distances with very little effort. You'll get your exercise chasing this model from one end of the room to the other.

Materials

* 8.5- by 11-inch (22- by 28-cm) paper

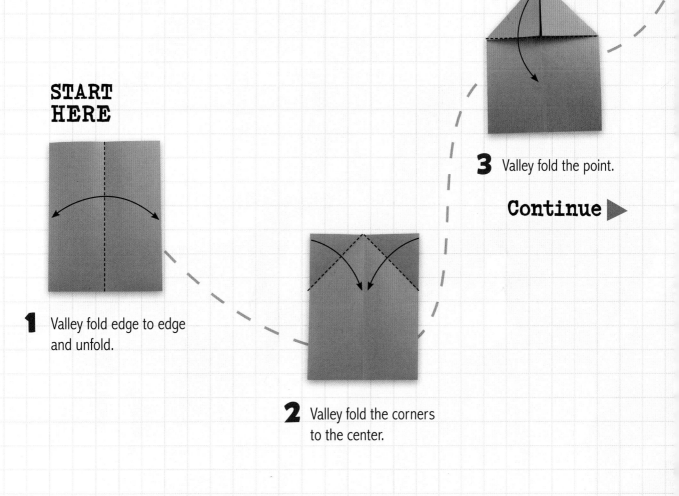

START HERE

1 Valley fold edge to edge and unfold.

2 Valley fold the corners to the center.

3 Valley fold the point.

Continue ▶

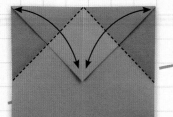

4 Valley fold the corners to the center and unfold.

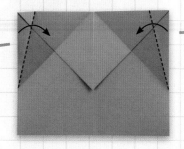

5 Valley fold the corners. Note that the creases end at the creases made in step 4.

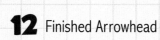

12 Finished Arrowhead

END HERE

11 Lift the wings.

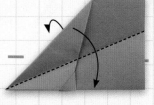

10 Valley fold the top flap even with the bottom edge. Repeat behind.

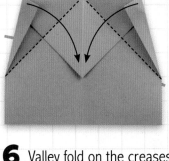

6 Valley fold on the creases made in step 4.

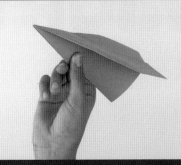
An airplane needs an upward force called lift to fly. Wings create lift as air flows over them during flight. Airplane wings are usually curved. Air molecules moving over the wing's top, curved surface travel faster than molecules moving along the wing's flat bottom. The slower-moving air molecules beneath the wing create a high amount of pressure and create lift.

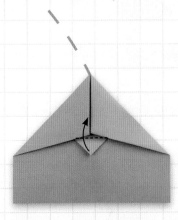

7 Valley fold the point.

8 Turn the model over.

9 Valley fold the model in half and rotate.

51

NIGHTHAWK

Traditional Model

The Nighthawk is a great flier with a simple design. This classic glider isn't fancy, but its graceful flight is sure to impress. Make two planes and challenge a friend to a flight contest.

Materials

* 8.5- by 11-inch (22- by 28-cm) paper

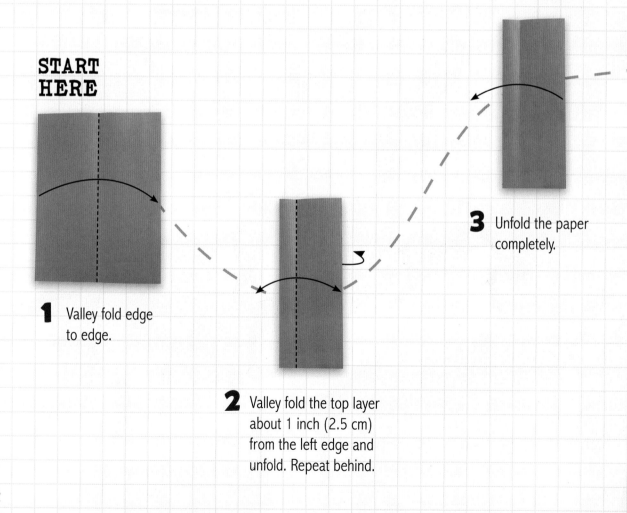

START HERE

1 Valley fold edge to edge.

2 Valley fold the top layer about 1 inch (2.5 cm) from the left edge and unfold. Repeat behind.

3 Unfold the paper completely.

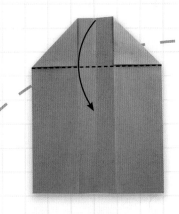

5 Valley fold the point.

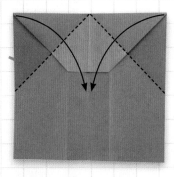

6 Valley fold the corners to the center crease.

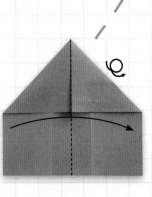

7 Valley fold the model in half and rotate.

4 Valley fold the corners to the creases made in step 2.

A glider is a small plane without an engine. It's often towed into the air by a rope connected to a motorized plane, then released into the sky. A glider uses air currents called thermals to stay aloft for hours. Thermals are special columns of warm, rising air, created by the sun's rays heating Earth's surface. Thermals push up on a glider's wings and keep it in flight.

8 Valley fold the top layer. Repeat behind.

Continue ▶

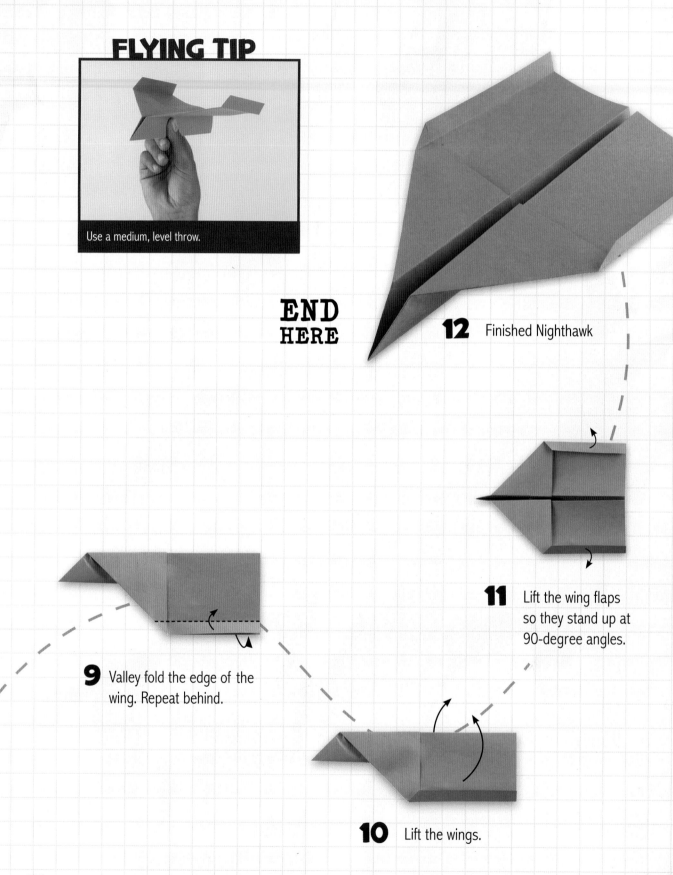

END HERE

FLYING TIP

Use a medium, level throw.

12 Finished Nighthawk

11 Lift the wing flaps so they stand up at 90-degree angles.

9 Valley fold the edge of the wing. Repeat behind.

10 Lift the wings.

VAPOR

Designed by Christopher L. Harbo

The Vapor has extra folds in the nose for strength and balance. The wing flaps guide the plane on an even flight. With very little effort, this model will slip silently from your hand and arc across the room.

Materials

* 8.5- by 11-inch (22- by 28-cm) paper

START HERE

1 Valley fold edge to edge and unfold.

2 Valley fold the corners to the center. Note how the creases end at the bottom corners of the paper.

3 Valley fold to point A.

Continue ▶

6 Valley fold the model in half and rotate.

5 Valley fold the corners to the center.

An airplane in flight rotates along three lines, or axes: lateral, vertical, and longitudinal. Movement along the lateral axis (which runs from wing to wing) is called pitch. The nose moves up or down. Movement along the vertical axis (which runs through the center of the plane) is called yaw. The nose moves side to side. When a plane moves around the longitudinal axis (which runs from nose to tail), the plane rolls.

4 Turn the model over.

FLYING TIP

Use a medium, smooth throw with a slight upward angle.

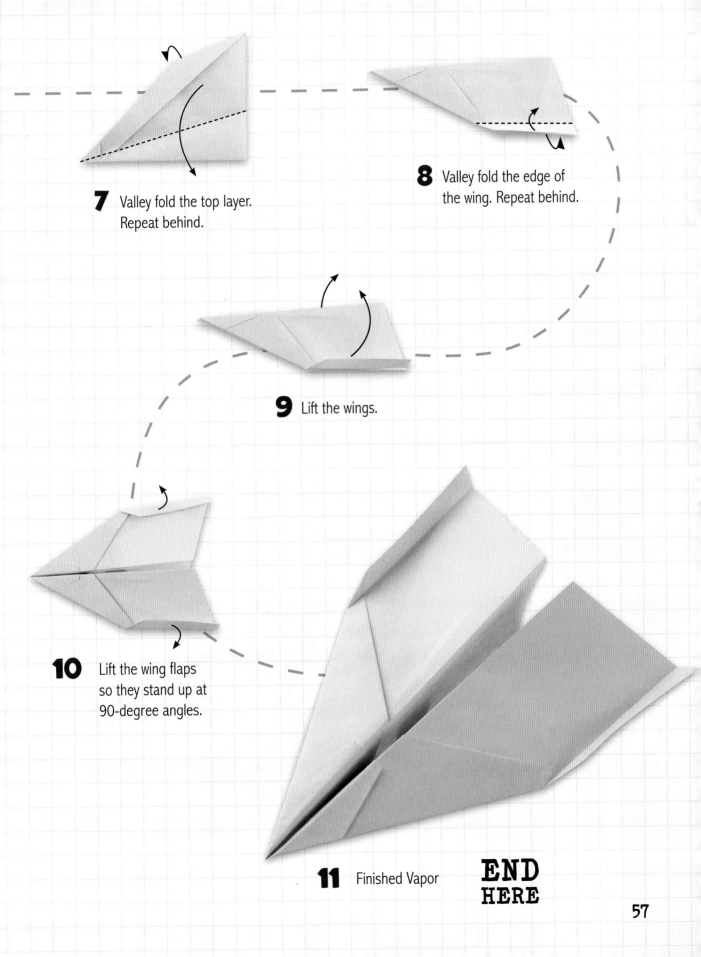

7 Valley fold the top layer. Repeat behind.

8 Valley fold the edge of the wing. Repeat behind.

9 Lift the wings.

10 Lift the wing flaps so they stand up at 90-degree angles.

11 Finished Vapor

END HERE

ADVANCED-LEVEL PROJECTS

Welcome aboard! You've earned the rank of pilot, and you're ready to fly. This is where the folding *really* gets fun. Plus, you get to use rubber bands and binder clips too! The following eight paper airplane projects might look tough at first, but you can do it.

Follow the instructions carefully, keep your creases sharp, and work at your own pace. When you need a break, check out the lightbulb boxes and refresh your knowledge of flight-science concepts.

LIFTOFF

Designed by Christopher L. Harbo

Ever wish you could put more power behind your launch? Your wish is granted with this plane. The notch in Liftoff's nose is strong enough to withstand the pull of a rubber band. Get ready. Aim. Fire away!

Materials

* 8.5- by 11-inch (22- by 28-cm) paper
* scissors
* rubber band

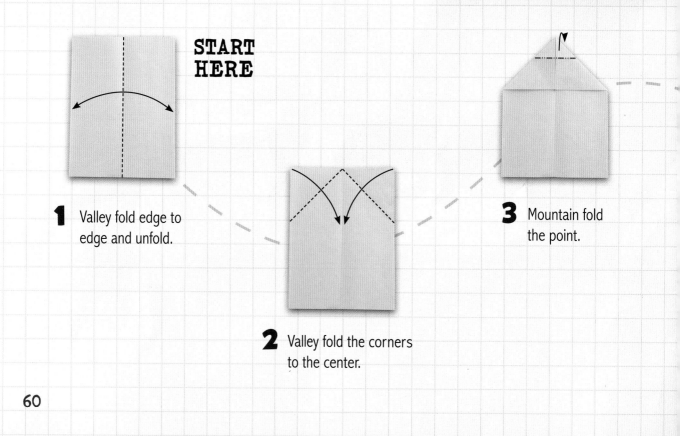

START HERE

1 Valley fold edge to edge and unfold.

2 Valley fold the corners to the center.

3 Mountain fold the point.

60

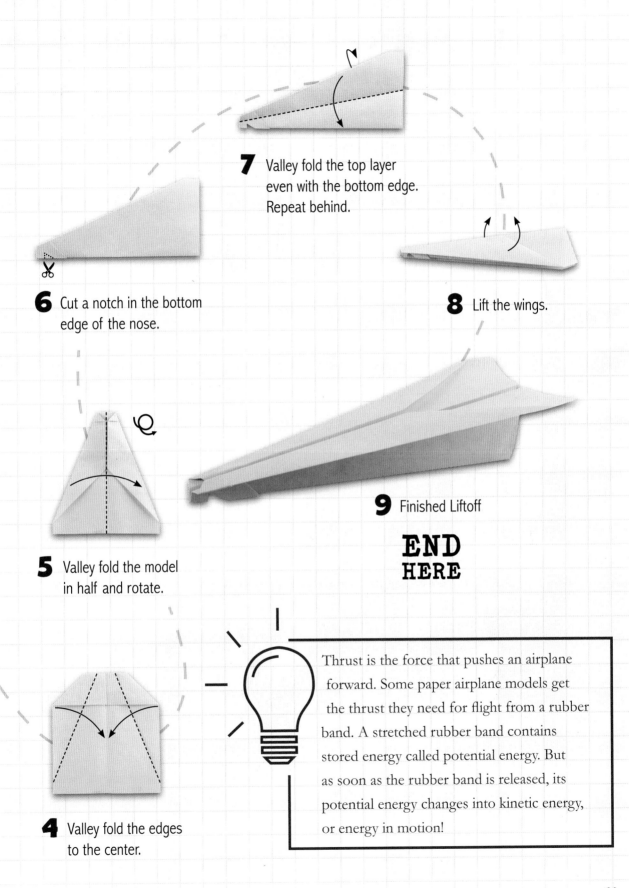

7 Valley fold the top layer even with the bottom edge. Repeat behind.

6 Cut a notch in the bottom edge of the nose.

8 Lift the wings.

9 Finished Liftoff

END HERE

5 Valley fold the model in half and rotate.

4 Valley fold the edges to the center.

Thrust is the force that pushes an airplane forward. Some paper airplane models get the thrust they need for flight from a rubber band. A stretched rubber band contains stored energy called potential energy. But as soon as the rubber band is released, its potential energy changes into kinetic energy, or energy in motion!

N E DL NOS

Traditional Model

It's not hard to figure out how the Needle Nose got its name. This model's pointy beak gets damaged easily. But the plane's awesome flights will make up for the time you spend straightening the nose.

Materials

* 8.5- by 11-inch (22- by 28-cm) paper

FLYING TIP

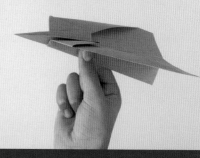

Use a medium throw with a slight upward angle.

START HERE

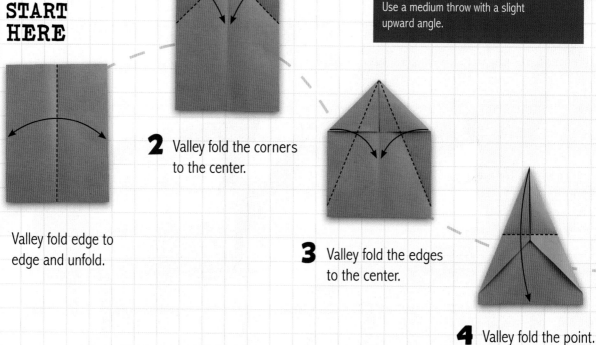

1 Valley fold edge to edge and unfold.

2 Valley fold the corners to the center.

3 Valley fold the edges to the center.

4 Valley fold the point.

62

As an airplane soars through the sky, a force called drag pushes against its forward movement. Drag is caused by air rubbing against a plane's surface. Airplanes with thin, sleek noses experience less drag upfront, which means a faster flight!

8 Lift the wings.

9 Finished Needle Nose

END HERE

7 Valley fold the top layer. Repeat behind.

6 Valley fold the model in half and rotate.

5 Valley fold the point. Note how the crease is even with point A.

AVIATOR

Traditional Model

The Aviator is one cool mini jet. This model looks like a dart and has a built-in cockpit. With a strong throw, you might think a tiny pilot is guiding it across the room.

Materials

* 6-inch (15-cm) square of paper

Most fighter jets have joysticks in the cockpit. A joystick is used to operate an airplane's ailerons and elevator. Ailerons are small, hinged fins on the end of wings that help a plane turn by rolling. An elevator is a moveable surface on a plane's tail. It causes up and down movement of the nose, called pitch.

START HERE

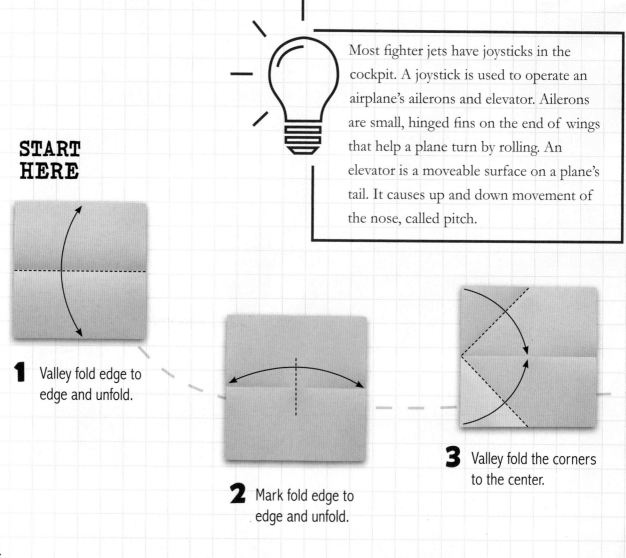

1 Valley fold edge to edge and unfold.

2 Mark fold edge to edge and unfold.

3 Valley fold the corners to the center.

5 Valley fold the edges to the center.

6 Mountain fold the model in half.

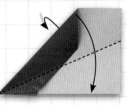

7 Valley fold the top layer even with the bottom edge. Repeat behind.

FLYING TIP

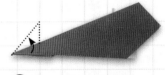

Use a strong throw with a slight upward angle.

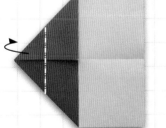

4 Mountain fold the point to the mark made in step 2.

8 Pull up the triangle in the nose to form a cockpit.

9 Lift the wings.

END HERE

10 Finished Aviator

FANG

Designed by Christopher L. Harbo

Tiny teeth give the Fang a dangerous look, but this gentle glider won't bite. The plane's light wings are at the mercy of air currents. In flight, it sways from side to side as it crosses a room.

Materials

* 8.5- by 11-inch (22- by 28-cm) paper

The weight of an airplane is the downward force that pulls it toward the ground. Lift is the upward force created by air moving around a plane's wings. Lift must be greater than weight for an airplane to take off and fly.

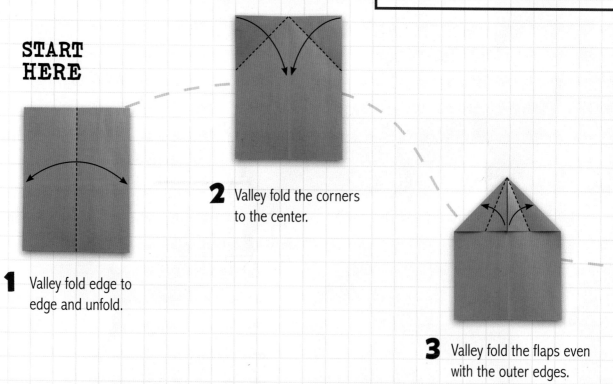

START HERE

1 Valley fold edge to edge and unfold.

2 Valley fold the corners to the center.

3 Valley fold the flaps even with the outer edges.

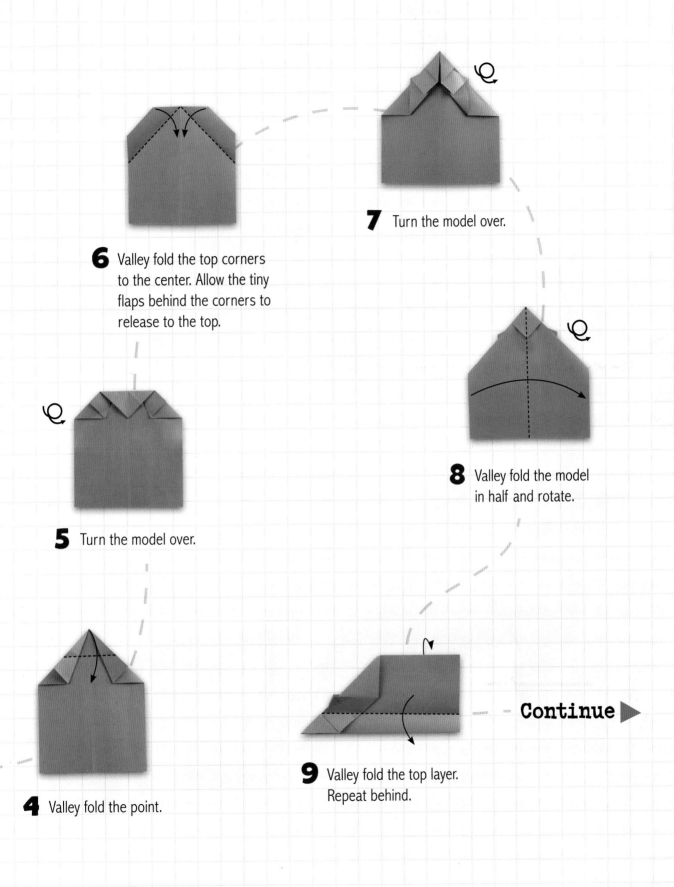

6 Valley fold the top corners to the center. Allow the tiny flaps behind the corners to release to the top.

7 Turn the model over.

8 Valley fold the model in half and rotate.

5 Turn the model over.

4 Valley fold the point.

9 Valley fold the top layer. Repeat behind.

Continue ▶

12 Finished Fang

END
HERE

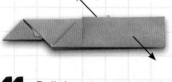

11 Pull the wings outward
to unfold.

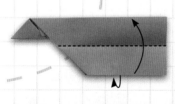

10 Valley fold the wing
even with the top edge.
Repeat behind.

FLYING TIP

Use a medium, level throw.

LAZY LANDER

Designed by Christopher L. Harbo

Make way for the Lazy Lander! This plane gets its magic from the binder clip. Placed under the nose, the clip gives the glider the weight it needs to fly. Better yet, the clip's legs can serve as landing gear.

Materials

* 8.5- by 11-inch (22- by 28-cm) paper
* small binder clip

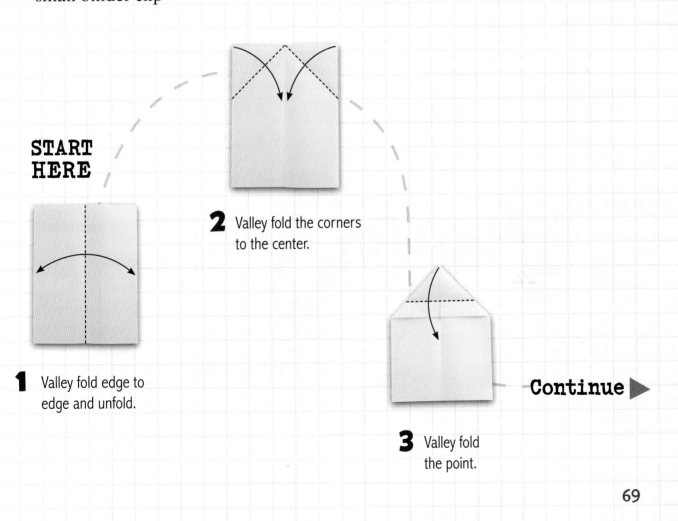

START HERE

1 Valley fold edge to edge and unfold.

2 Valley fold the corners to the center.

3 Valley fold the point.

Continue ▶

7 Valley fold the top layer. Repeat behind.

6 Valley fold the model in half and rotate.

8 Valley fold the edge of the wing. Repeat behind.

5 Valley fold the point.

9 Valley fold the wing flap even with the bottom edge. Repeat behind.

4 Valley fold the point.

Most airplanes have wheels to create a smooth landing for passengers. Plane wheels are equipped with shock absorbers, which allow the wheels to move up and down to lessen the landing impact. Shock absorbers change kinetic energy (energy in motion) into another type of energy: heat.

END HERE

13 Finished Lazy Lander

FLYING TIP

Use a medium, level throw.

12 Add a binder clip to the front of the plane.

10 Lift the wings.

11 Pull the wing flaps up and out to the side.

HANG GLIDER

Traditional Model

The Hang Glider takes you soaring to new heights.
With the right throw, this glider climbs into the air.
When it can go no higher, it banks to the side and
curves around the room.

Materials

* 10-inch (25-cm) square of paper

START HERE

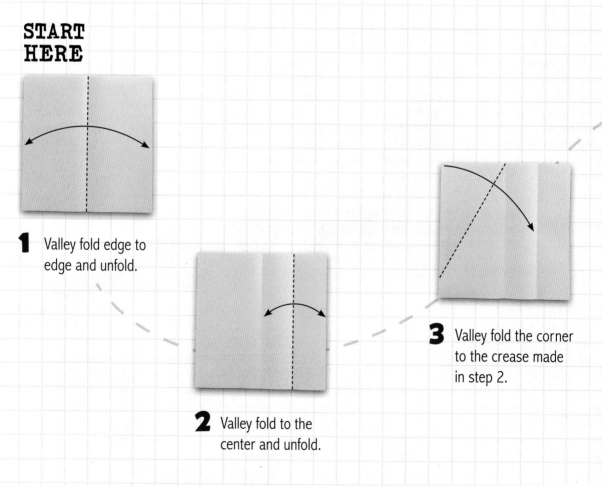

1 Valley fold edge to edge and unfold.

2 Valley fold to the center and unfold.

3 Valley fold the corner to the crease made in step 2.

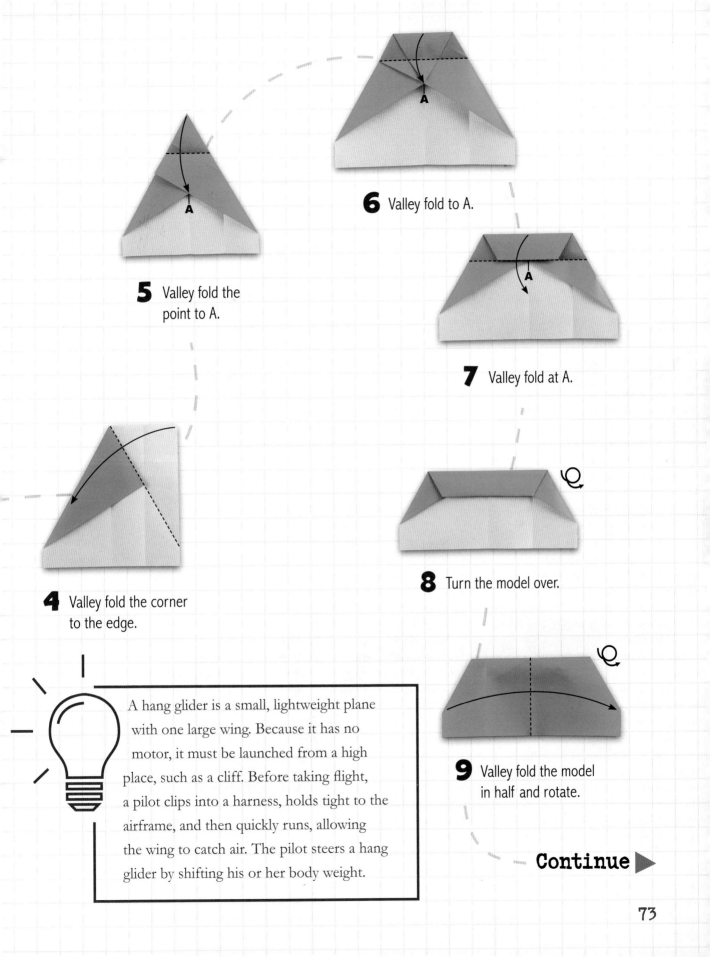

6 Valley fold to A.

5 Valley fold the point to A.

7 Valley fold at A.

4 Valley fold the corner to the edge.

8 Turn the model over.

A hang glider is a small, lightweight plane with one large wing. Because it has no motor, it must be launched from a high place, such as a cliff. Before taking flight, a pilot clips into a harness, holds tight to the airframe, and then quickly runs, allowing the wing to catch air. The pilot steers a hang glider by shifting his or her body weight.

9 Valley fold the model in half and rotate.

Continue ▶

12 Lift the wings.

13 Lift the wing flaps so they stand up at 90-degree angles.

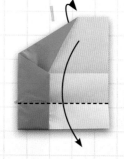

11 Valley fold the edge of the wing. Repeat behind.

14 Finished Hang Glider

END
HERE

10 Valley fold the top layer. Repeat behind.

FLYING TIP

Use a medium throw with a slight upward angle.

ST ADY DDI

Designed by Christopher L. Harbo

Get ready for the Steady Eddie. Broad wings and slim wing flaps give this glider a smooth, stable flight. Two small paper clips beside the nose help guide the craft as it comes in for a landing.

Materials

* 8.5- by 11-inch (22- by 28-cm) paper
* two small paper clips

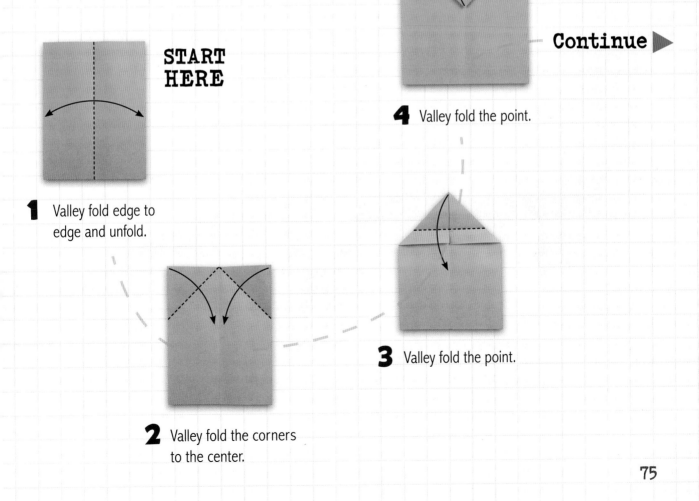

START HERE

1 Valley fold edge to edge and unfold.

2 Valley fold the corners to the center.

3 Valley fold the point.

4 Valley fold the point.

Continue ▶

75

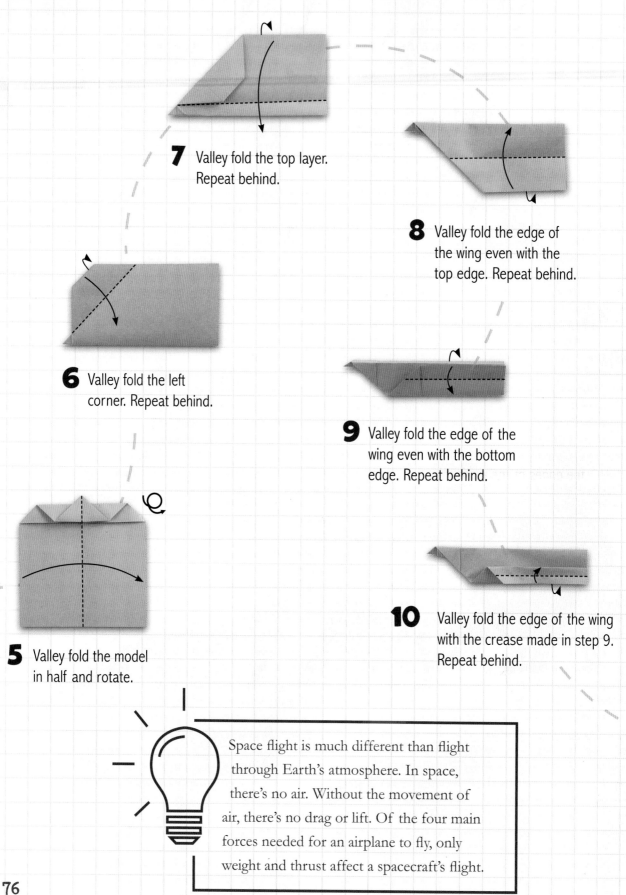

7 Valley fold the top layer. Repeat behind.

8 Valley fold the edge of the wing even with the top edge. Repeat behind.

6 Valley fold the left corner. Repeat behind.

9 Valley fold the edge of the wing even with the bottom edge. Repeat behind.

5 Valley fold the model in half and rotate.

10 Valley fold the edge of the wing with the crease made in step 9. Repeat behind.

Space flight is much different than flight through Earth's atmosphere. In space, there's no air. Without the movement of air, there's no drag or lift. Of the four main forces needed for an airplane to fly, only weight and thrust affect a spacecraft's flight.

Use a medium throw with a steep upward angle.

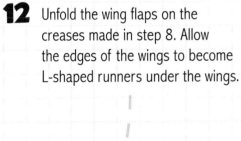

13 Turn the model over.

12 Unfold the wing flaps on the creases made in step 8. Allow the edges of the wings to become L-shaped runners under the wings.

14 Attach a small paper clip to each side of the nose. Turn the model over.

11 Lift the wings.

15 Finished Steady Eddie

END HERE

D-WING

Traditional Model

The D-wing's flight depends on how you release it. One flight might be long, smooth, and straight. The next might wobble, curve, and dive. It's a model that will keep you guessing.

Materials

* 8.5- by 11-inch (22- by 28-cm) paper

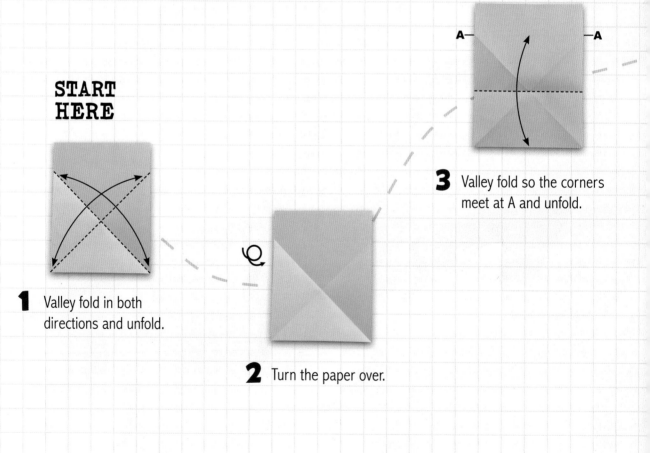

START HERE

1 Valley fold in both directions and unfold.

2 Turn the paper over.

3 Valley fold so the corners meet at A and unfold.

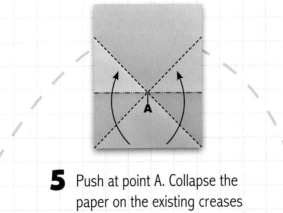

5 Push at point A. Collapse the paper on the existing creases to form a triangle.

4 Turn the paper over.

6 Valley fold the top layers to the point and unfold.

7 Mountain fold the top layers on the creases made in step 6.

8 Valley fold the model in half and unfold.

Continue ▶

Earth's gravity is the force that is constantly pulling objects with mass (including people) to the ground. Whenever someone slams on the brakes, blasts off in a rocket, or takes a sharp turn in a jet, he or she changes speed faster than gravity can pull. The measure of the change in speed is called g-force. High g-forces can be deadly. A person standing at sea level feels 1 G. Many race car drivers feel 5 Gs. Fighter jet pilots wearing special g-suits can endure 8 or 9 Gs.

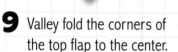

9 Valley fold the corners of the top flap to the center.

10 Valley fold the point and unfold.

11 Tuck the flaps into the pockets of the point.

FLYING TIP

Pinch the back of the wing with two fingers and your thumb. The model will bend upward in the middle. Release with a strong forward flick of the wrist.

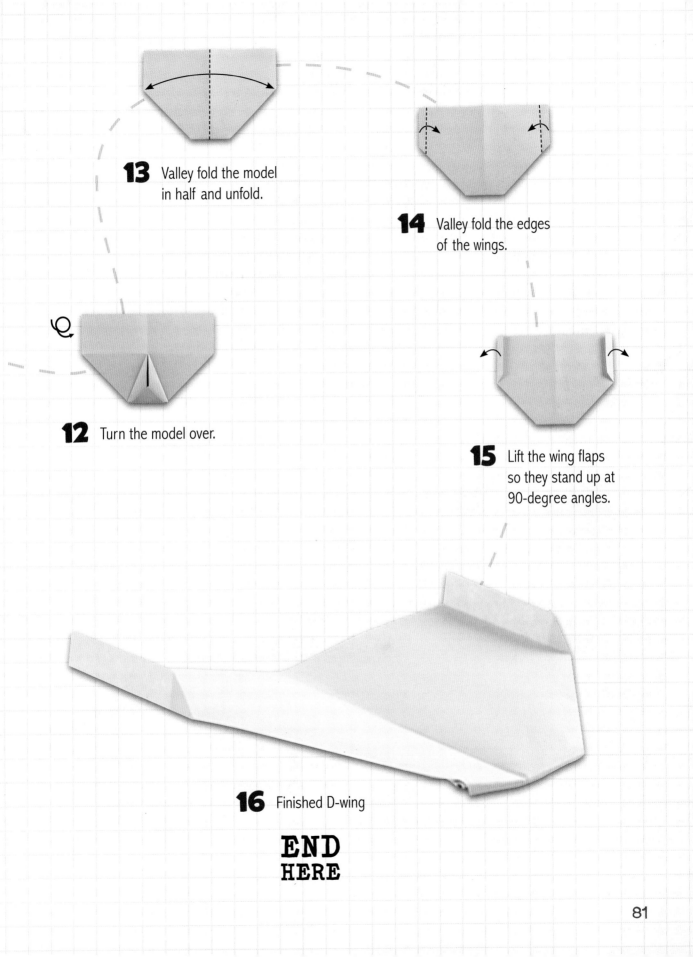

13 Valley fold the model in half and unfold.

14 Valley fold the edges of the wings.

12 Turn the model over.

15 Lift the wing flaps so they stand up at 90-degree angles.

16 Finished D-wing

END HERE

EXPERT-LEVEL PROJECTS

Congratulations on making the rank of captain!

You have hours of flight experience under your belt.

Now it's time to take command. The seven

paper airplane projects in this section are

for highly skilled pilots only—that's you!

Try the sleek Fighter Jet or the snub-nosed Warthog. How about the crazy Flying Accordion or the fierce Screech Owl? They won't be easy to fold, but once they're done, they'll be some of the most awesome paper planes you'll ever fly.

FIGHTER JET

Traditional Model

Want a fighter jet that is always ready for its next military mission? This stylish plane swoops through the air. It's a great flier that looks super cool.

Materials

* 6.5- by 11-inch (16.5- by 28-cm) paper

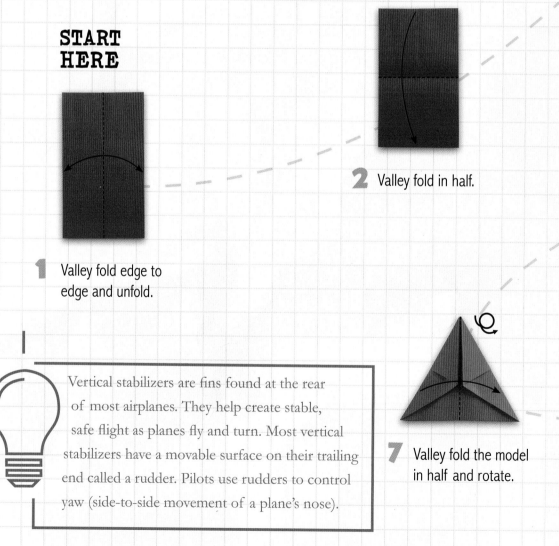

START HERE

1 Valley fold edge to edge and unfold.

2 Valley fold in half.

Vertical stabilizers are fins found at the rear of most airplanes. They help create stable, safe flight as planes fly and turn. Most vertical stabilizers have a movable surface on their trailing end called a rudder. Pilots use rudders to control yaw (side-to-side movement of a plane's nose).

7 Valley fold the model in half and rotate.

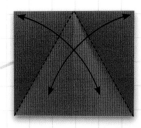

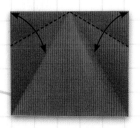

3 Valley fold the corners and unfold. Note how creases run from the center to the bottom corners.

4 Valley fold the corners to the creases made in step 3 and unfold.

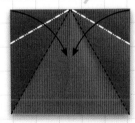

5 Squash fold using the creases made in steps 3 and 4.

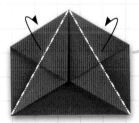

6 Mountain fold on the existing creases.

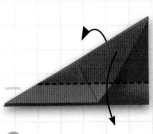

8 Valley fold the top layer. Repeat behind.

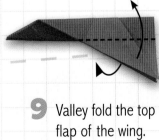

9 Valley fold the top flap of the wing. Repeat behind.

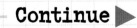

Continue ▶

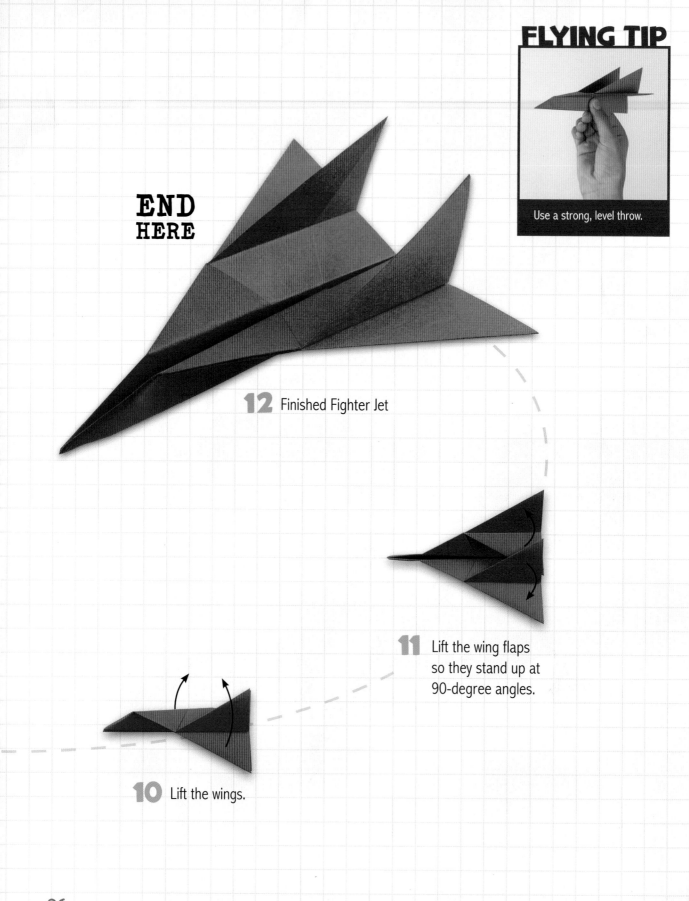

END
HERE

12 Finished Fighter Jet

11 Lift the wing flaps
so they stand up at
90-degree angles.

10 Lift the wings.

WARTHOG

Designed by Christopher L. Harbo

The Warthog is a beast. It may not be pretty, but this little glider soars long distances through the air. Don't worry about hitting the wall. The Warthog's snub nose can take a beating.

Materials

* 8.5- by 11-inch (22- by 28-cm) paper

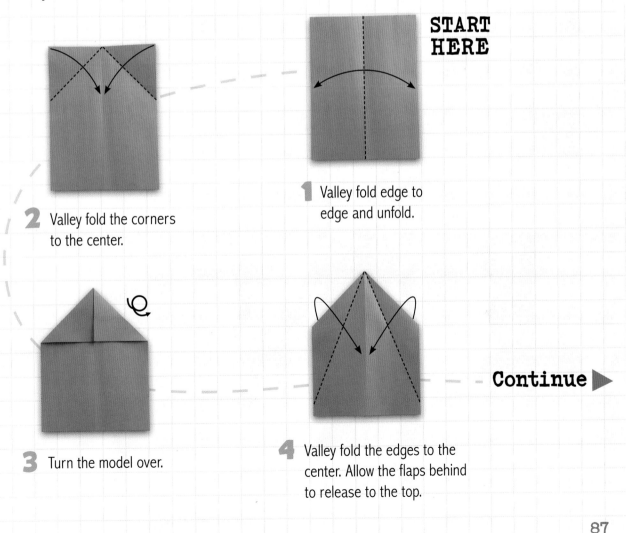

START HERE

1 Valley fold edge to edge and unfold.

2 Valley fold the corners to the center.

3 Turn the model over.

4 Valley fold the edges to the center. Allow the flaps behind to release to the top.

Continue ▶

87

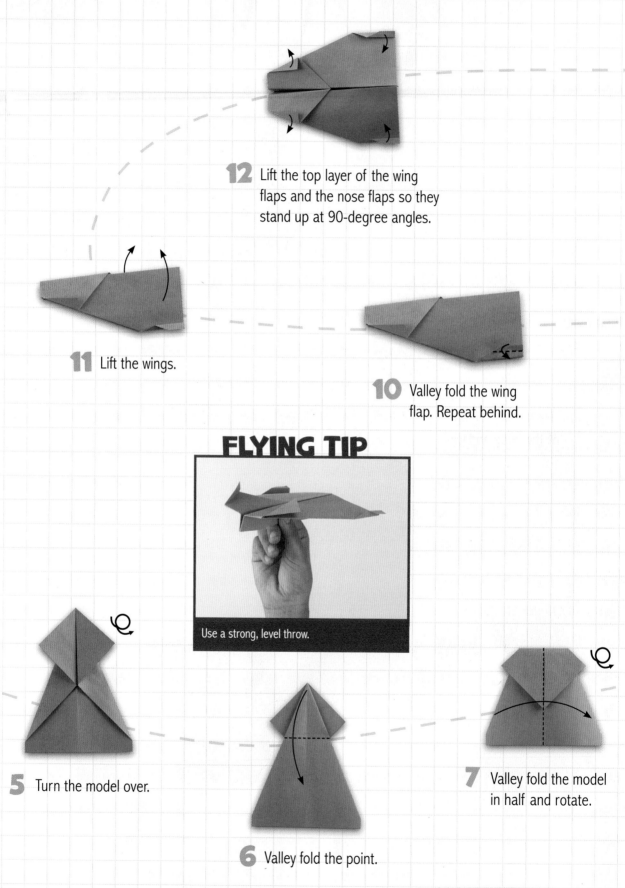

12 Lift the top layer of the wing flaps and the nose flaps so they stand up at 90-degree angles.

11 Lift the wings.

10 Valley fold the wing flap. Repeat behind.

FLYING TIP

Use a strong, level throw.

5 Turn the model over.

6 Valley fold the point.

7 Valley fold the model in half and rotate.

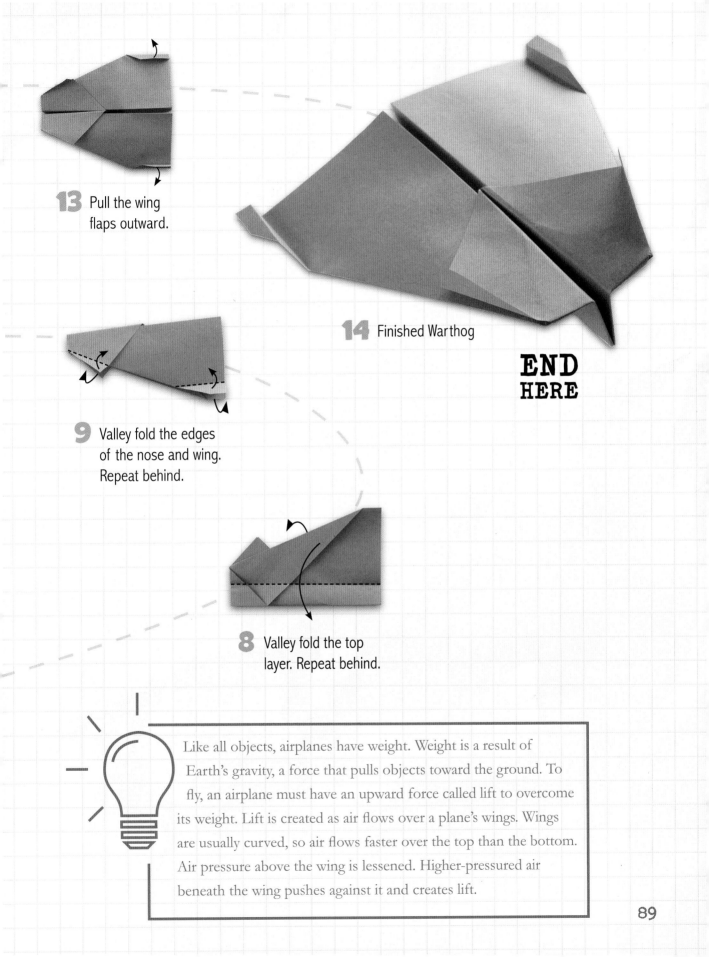

13 Pull the wing flaps outward.

14 Finished Warthog

END HERE

9 Valley fold the edges of the nose and wing. Repeat behind.

8 Valley fold the top layer. Repeat behind.

Like all objects, airplanes have weight. Weight is a result of Earth's gravity, a force that pulls objects toward the ground. To fly, an airplane must have an upward force called lift to overcome its weight. Lift is created as air flows over a plane's wings. Wings are usually curved, so air flows faster over the top than the bottom. Air pressure above the wing is lessened. Higher-pressured air beneath the wing pushes against it and creates lift.

GLIDING GRACE

Designed by Christopher L. Harbo

Flying the Gliding Grace takes a soft touch. Throw it too hard and it goes into a steep dive. But a smooth, medium throw sends this model soaring. It's the perfect plane to practice your launching skills.

Materials

* 8.5- by 11-inch (22- by 28-cm) paper

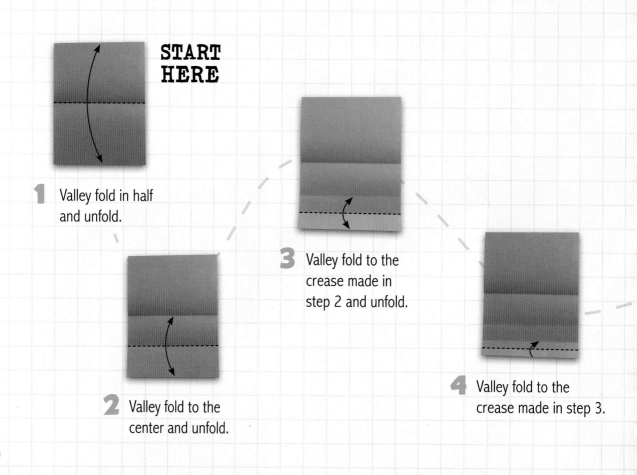

START HERE

1 Valley fold in half and unfold.

2 Valley fold to the center and unfold.

3 Valley fold to the crease made in step 2 and unfold.

4 Valley fold to the crease made in step 3.

7 Valley fold on the crease made in step 2.

8 Turn the model over.

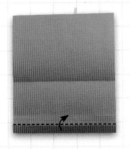

6 Valley fold to the crease made in step 2.

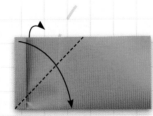

9 Valley fold the model in half and rotate.

10 Valley fold the left edge to the bottom edge. Repeat behind.

5 Valley fold on the crease made in step 3.

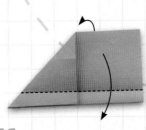

11 Valley fold the top layer. Repeat behind.

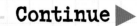

Continue ▶

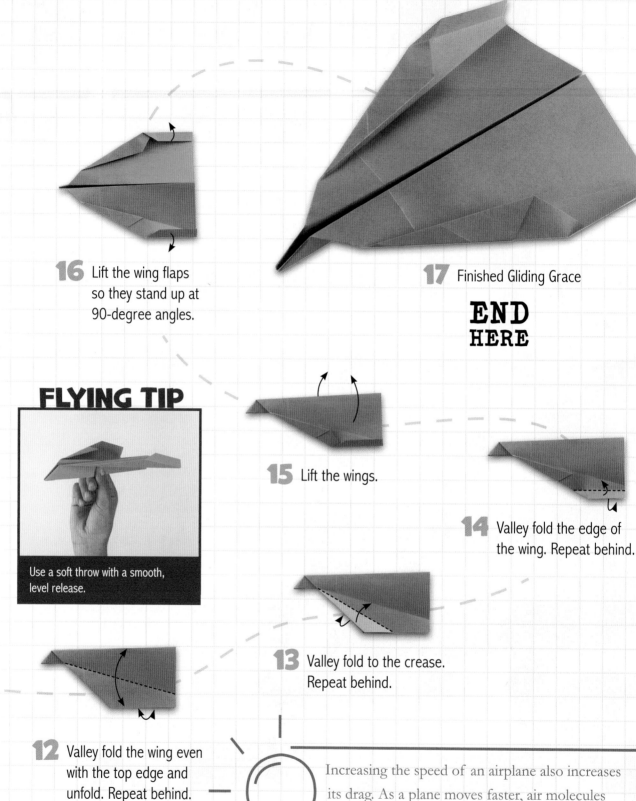

16 Lift the wing flaps so they stand up at 90-degree angles.

17 Finished Gliding Grace

END HERE

15 Lift the wings.

14 Valley fold the edge of the wing. Repeat behind.

FLYING TIP

Use a soft throw with a smooth, level release.

13 Valley fold to the crease. Repeat behind.

12 Valley fold the wing even with the top edge and unfold. Repeat behind.

Increasing the speed of an airplane also increases its drag. As a plane moves faster, air molecules have a more difficult time moving out of the plane's way. Just like snow piles up in front of a snowplow, air molecules pile up near a wing's front edge at fast speeds and create drag.

FLYING ACCORDION

Traditional Model

Can a paper plane with so many peaks and valleys really fly? Fold the Flying Accordion and find out. This unique glider will have your friends begging you to make them one.

Materials

* 8.5- by 11-inch (22- by 28-cm) paper

START HERE

1 Valley fold edge to edge and unfold.

2 Turn the paper over.

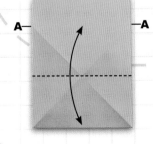

3 Valley fold so the corners meet at point A and unfold.

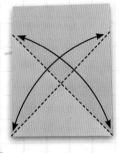

4 Turn the paper over.

Continue ▶

10 Repeat steps 6 through 9 on the left side.

11 Mountain fold the point.

9 Rabbit ear fold on the creases formed in steps 7 and 8.

FLYING TIP

Pinch the plane on the triangle beneath its wings. Give it a medium, level throw.

8 Valley fold to the center and unfold.

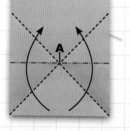

5 Push at point A. Collapse the paper on the existing creases to form a triangle.

7 Valley fold to the center and unfold.

6 Valley fold the top layer to the point.

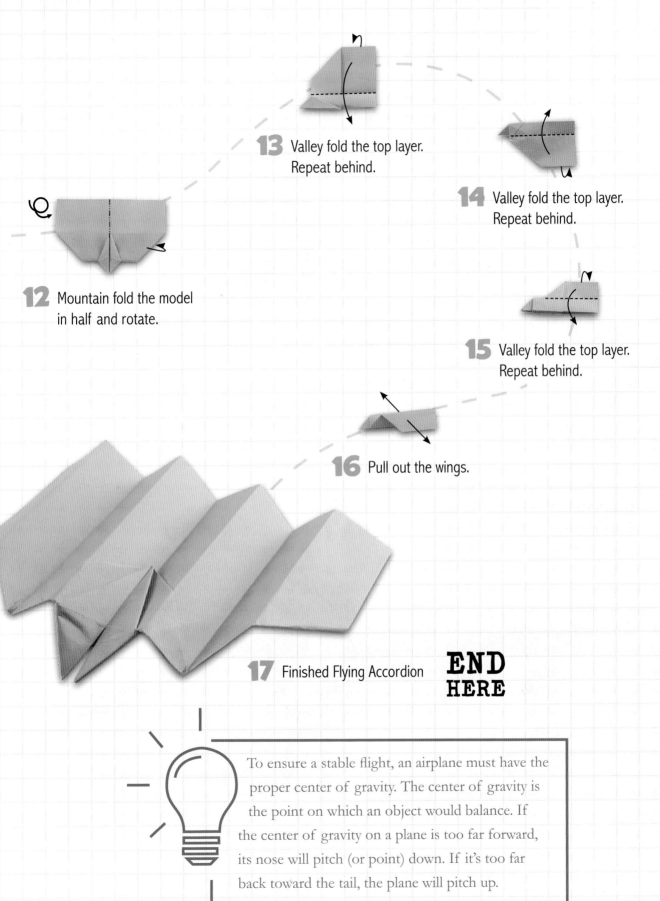

13 Valley fold the top layer. Repeat behind.

14 Valley fold the top layer. Repeat behind.

12 Mountain fold the model in half and rotate.

15 Valley fold the top layer. Repeat behind.

16 Pull out the wings.

17 Finished Flying Accordion

END HERE

To ensure a stable flight, an airplane must have the proper center of gravity. The center of gravity is the point on which an object would balance. If the center of gravity on a plane is too far forward, its nose will pitch (or point) down. If it's too far back toward the tail, the plane will pitch up.

SPACE BOMBER

Traditional Model

The Space Bomber looks like it flew in from another world. Don't let this plane's boxy shape fool you. Its flight paths are amazingly straight and long.

Materials

* 8.5- by 11-inch (22- by 28-cm) paper

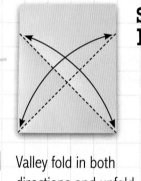

START HERE

1 Valley fold in both directions and unfold.

2 Turn the paper over.

3 Valley fold so the corners meet at point A and unfold.

4 Turn the paper over.

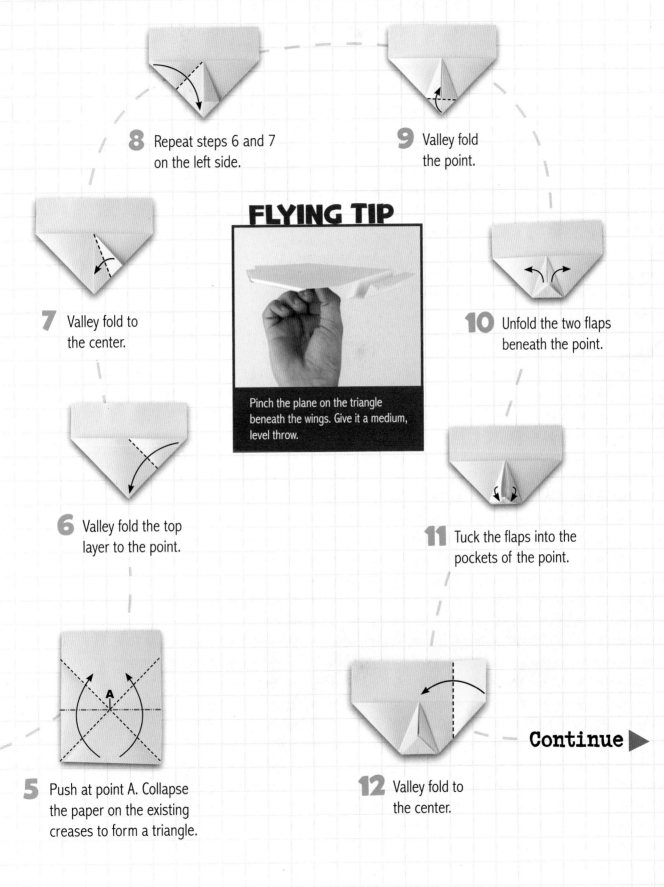

8 Repeat steps 6 and 7 on the left side.

9 Valley fold the point.

FLYING TIP

Pinch the plane on the triangle beneath the wings. Give it a medium, level throw.

7 Valley fold to the center.

10 Unfold the two flaps beneath the point.

6 Valley fold the top layer to the point.

11 Tuck the flaps into the pockets of the point.

5 Push at point A. Collapse the paper on the existing creases to form a triangle.

A

12 Valley fold to the center.

Continue ▶

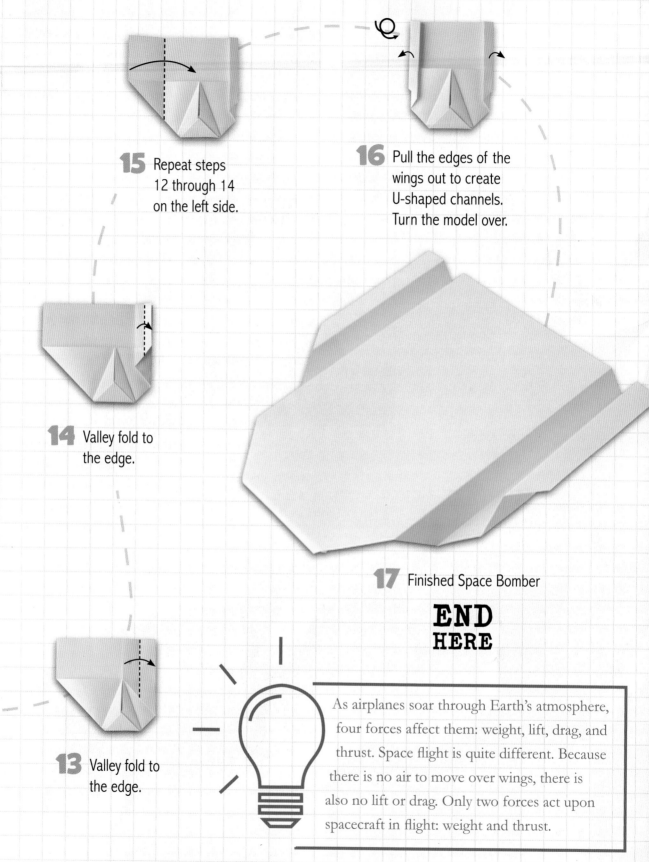

15 Repeat steps 12 through 14 on the left side.

16 Pull the edges of the wings out to create U-shaped channels. Turn the model over.

14 Valley fold to the edge.

17 Finished Space Bomber

END HERE

13 Valley fold to the edge.

As airplanes soar through Earth's atmosphere, four forces affect them: weight, lift, drag, and thrust. Space flight is quite different. Because there is no air to move over wings, there is also no lift or drag. Only two forces act upon spacecraft in flight: weight and thrust.

SPARROWHAWK

Traditional Model

Do you want the Sparrowhawk to sail like a glider or loop around like a stunt plane? Changing the power and angle of your throw will determine how this plane flies. Either way, the Sparrowhawk doesn't disappoint.

Materials

* 8.5- by 11-inch (22- by 28-cm) paper

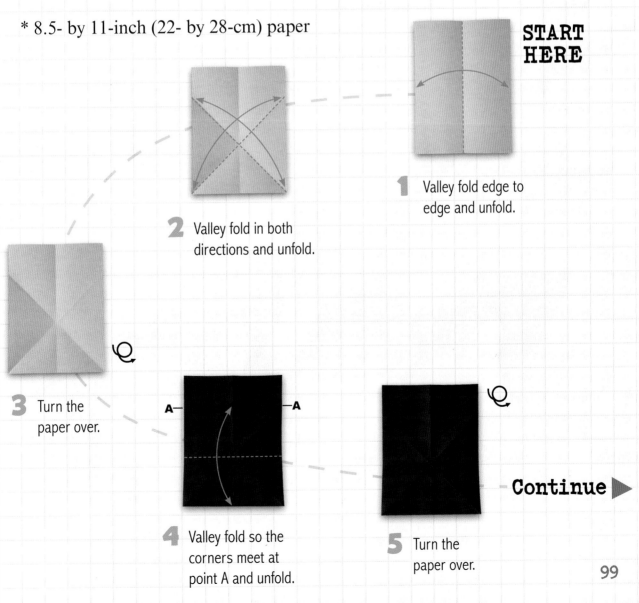

START HERE

1 Valley fold edge to edge and unfold.

2 Valley fold in both directions and unfold.

3 Turn the paper over.

4 Valley fold so the corners meet at point A and unfold.

5 Turn the paper over.

Continue ▶

9 Valley fold to the center and unfold.

8 Valley fold to the center and unfold.

10 Rabbit ear fold on the creases formed in steps 8 and 9.

7 Valley fold the top layer to the point.

11 Repeat steps 7 through 10 on the left side.

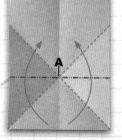

A

6 Push at point A. Collapse the paper on the existing creases to form a triangle.

All airplanes need a force called thrust to fly. Gas- and electric-powered engines produce thrust for full-size planes. The push of a hand or a rubber-band launcher gives paper airplanes the thrust they need. Hang gliders get thrust from their pilots running and often jumping from a hill or cliff.

**END
HERE**

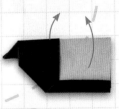

18 Finished Sparrowhawk

12 Mountain fold
the point.

FLYING TIP

For smooth flights, give the plane
a medium, level throw. For stunt
flights, give it a hard throw with
a steep upward angle.

17 Lift the wing flaps
so they stand up at
90-degree angles.

13 Valley fold the
model in half
and rotate.

16 Lift the wings.

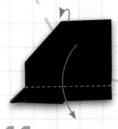

14 Valley fold
the top layer.
Repeat behind.

15 Valley fold
the top layer.
Repeat behind.

SCREECH OWL

Traditional Model

With its wide wings and narrow tail, the Screech Owl glides like a silent hunter. Hold it as high as you can to get the longest flight.

Materials

* 7- by 10.5-inch (18- by 27-cm) paper
* scissors

START HERE

1 Cut a 2-inch (5-cm) strip off the end of the paper.

2 Valley fold the strip edge to edge and unfold.

3 Valley fold the corners of the strip to the center. Set aside.

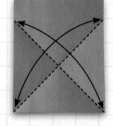

4 Valley fold the large paper in both directions and unfold.

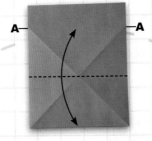

6 Valley fold so the corners meet at point A and unfold.

5 Turn the paper over.

7 Turn the paper over.

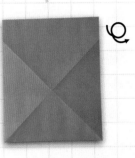

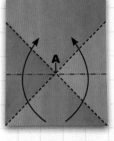

8 Push at point A. Collapse the paper on the existing creases to form a triangle.

Engineers have studied owl wings to learn how to design quieter airplanes. They discovered an owl wing has tiny hooks on its leading edge (the edge the wind hits first). These hooks create micro-turbulences that help the wing glide through the air with less friction—and, therefore, less noise.

Continue ▶

13 Repeat steps 9 through 12 on the left side.

14 Insert the strip between the layers so it fits in the point.

FLYING TIP

Pinch the triangle beneath the wings. Release by giving the plane a gentle push forward.

12 Rabbit ear fold on the creases formed in steps 10 and 11.

11 Valley fold to the center and unfold.

10 Valley fold to the center and unfold.

9 Valley fold the top layer to the point.

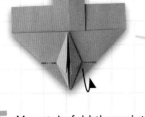

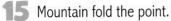

15 Mountain fold the point.

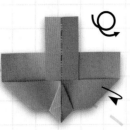

16 Mountain fold the model in half and rotate.

A bird's tail feathers provide stability during takeoff and landing. Tail feathers are also used for steering during flight. A bird can change direction by slightly twisting its tail. When it wants to slow down, it may spread its tail feathers to create more drag.

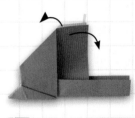

17 Lower the wings.

18 Finished Screech Owl

END HERE

INSIDE THE HANGAR

As cool as the paper airplanes in this book are, they can't beat the real thing! Let's take a look at some of the planes that have moved (and continue to move) people through the skies and how they came to be. Get the scoop on the Wright brothers . . . peek inside a wind tunnel . . . and take flight with a hang glider, paraglider, and stealth bomber.

THE WRIGHT BROTHERS' 1902 GLIDER

Two American brothers, Wilbur and Orville Wright, invented the first fully controllable aircraft in the world—the 1902 glider. But their journey to create this incredible flying craft was filled with unexpected problems and lots of crash landings! One of the biggest challenges the Wright brothers faced was finding a reliable way to control the craft's steering. After many test flights, they decided to try a rear rudder. (A plane rudder acts much like the rudder on a ship—it controls the direction of the craft.) Fortunately, their clever rudder idea worked. Finally, the pilot could control his craft in three directions: roll (up and down movement of the wing tips), pitch (up and down movement of the plane's nose), and yaw (side to side movement of the plane's nose).

The Wright brothers' glider had two 32-foot (9.8-m) wings. It didn't have any seats. Instead, the pilot lay down on the bottom wing and held tight to the controls. Built out of wood and strong fabric, the Wright brothers' glider weighed only 117 pounds (53 kilograms).

The 1902 glider was the first of the Wright brothers' gliders to include a rudder.

WIND TUNNELS

Engineers are people who use science and math to plan, design, or build. When creating new aircraft (or spacecraft), engineers often rely on wind tunnels to test their designs. A wind tunnel is a large tube-shaped piece of equipment. A mount in the center of the tube holds a test plane in place. When the wind tunnel is turned on, air flows around the plane like it would if the plane were flying.

Most wind tunnels have powerful fans to create high-speed winds. Air speeds in some tunnels reach 4,000 miles (6,437 kilometers) per hour—five times the speed of sound! During testing, smoke or dye may be injected into the wind so engineers can study how air flows around an airplane. Photographs of this moving air allow engineers to see how they can improve a plane's design to lower drag and increase lift.

To save money, engineers may test a smaller-scale model of a new plane design inside a smaller wind tunnel. Based on the engineers' findings, the design may be changed and tested again.

This seven-story wind tunnel was used to test airplane design in 1932.

HANG GLIDERS AND PARAGLIDERS

Although a hang glider doesn't have an engine to produce thrust, this small flying craft can soar for hours. Made of a lightweight metal frame and canvas, it has a high lift-to-drag ratio. This means that the amount of lift created by the glider's wing is far greater than the drag created by the glider and its pilot.

Areas with consistently hot, dry weather are the best places for hang gliders to take long flights. When the sun's rays heat up the ground, the air above it expands and rises. The rising columns of air are called thermals. Thermals push up on a hang glider's wing and keep the craft in flight.

The Guinness world record for the longest hang glider flight is 474.7 miles (764 km). The pilot, Dustin Martin, made his incredible 11-hour flight from Zapata, Texas, to Lubbock, Texas, on July 3, 2012.

A hang glider is really one big wing.

A paraglider is similar to a hang glider. Both use thermals to fly, move at about the same speed, and are relatively easy to control. The biggest difference is that a hang glider has a rigid frame, whereas a paraglider is simply a harness hanging from a fabric wing.

The B-2 Spirit stealth bomber is a flying-wing airplane. As its name suggests, it looks like a big wing, without a definite body (fuselage) or tail. It measures 172 feet (52 m) from wingtip to wingtip—about as long as an Olympic-sized swimming pool.

This powerful craft gets its thrust from four turbofan engines tucked inside its wings. It's designed to fly more than 6,000 nautical miles (6,905 miles; 11,112 km) without refueling. (Note: Nautical miles are the standard measurement for air and sea travel. They're slightly longer than land miles.)

Perhaps the coolest part of the B-2 stealth bomber is its ability to hide. It's the perfect spy plane! Two design features work together to make the bomber difficult to see on radar. First, a radar-absorbent coating covers the exterior of the plane. The coating "eats" the radar signals so they can't report back. Second, the plane's shape is designed with a technique called continuous curvature. Radar signals bounce off the curved surface, into all sorts of directions.

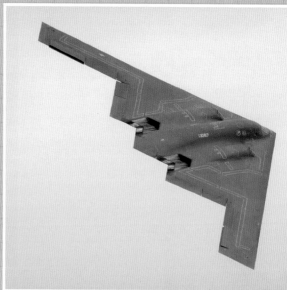

Flying-wing aircraft, such as the B-2 Spirit stealth bomber, house all of their crew, fuel, and equipment inside one giant wing structure.

NOT READY TO LAND YET?

Keep flying by checking out these paper-folding
and flight-related titles!

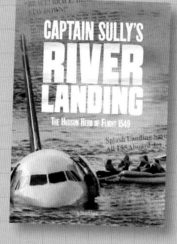

DC Super Heroes Origami,
by John Montroll
(ISBN: 9781623702175)

*Captain Sully's River Landing:
The Hudson Hero of Flight 1549,*
by Steven Otfinoski
(ISBN: 9781543541991)

*TV Brings the Moon
Landing to Earth,*
by Rebecca Rissman
(ISBN: 9780756560034)

Special thanks to our adviser, Polly Kadolph, Associate Professor, University of Dubuque (Iowa) Aviation Department, for her expertise.

Dabble Lab Books are published by Capstone Press, an imprint of Capstone.
1710 Roe Crest Drive, North Mankato, Minnesota 56003
www.capstonepub.com

Library of Congress Cataloging-in-Publication Data is available on the Library of Congress website.
ISBN 978-1-5435-0806-2 (paperback)

Summary: It's equal parts stunt-plane fun and aviator cool for builders of all levels! With step-by-step, photo-illustrated instructions, this collection of paper airplane projects shows readers how to fold a wild collection of gliders, blimps, jets, and whirlies, and pairs those projects with clear, concise explanations of the basic physics of flight.

Image Credits
Capstone Studio: Karon Dubke, all steps; Library of Congress, 107; Shutterstock: Alexandra Lande, 109, AMMHPhotography, 110, Everett Historical, 108

Design Elements
Capstone and Shutterstock

Editorial Credits
Jill Kalz, editor; Heidi Thompson and Kyle Grenz, designers; Eric Gohl, media researcher; Laura Manthe, production specialist

Printed and bound in China. PO5716